RAISING PEACEMAKERS

RAISING PEACEMAKERS

ESTHER SOKOLOV FINE

GARN PRESS
NEW YORK, NY

Published by Garn Press, LLC
New York, NY
www.garnpress.com

Book and cover design by Benjamin J. Taylor/Garn Press
Cover drawing by Lena Kahn, used with permission

Library of Congress Control Number: 2015936441

Publisher's Cataloging-in-Publication Data

Esther Sokolov Fine
Raising Peacemakers / Esther Sokolov Fine.
pages cm
Includes bibliographical references.
ISBN: 978-1-942146-12-4 (pbk.)
ISBN: 978-1-942146-19-3 (hardcover)
ISBN: 978-1-942146-13-1 (e-book)
1. Children and peace. 2. Empathy in children. 3. Affective education. 4. Interpersonal conflict in children. 5. Peer mediation. 6. Downtown Alternative School (Toronto, Ont.) I. Title.
LB1027.5 .F5 2015
371.5`9—dc23

2015936441

This book is dedicated to the children and teachers at Downtown Alternative School, past, present, and future. Eternal thanks go to Joan Baer, Ann Lacey, Lori McCubbin and Marie Lardino, four brilliant teachers who helped children invent, articulate, and sustain peacemaking.

We remember with love and admiration Adrian Adamson, Ron Squire, Jim Milner, Jeremy Loomes, and Tashi McGowan.

Acknowledgements

Roberta King and Ron Squire (King Squire Films Ltd.) filmed the first three years of this study from 1993 to 1996. Their astonishing talents and hard work in that early phase made it possible to document and share peacemaking from that time to this. My appreciation for their work goes far beyond anything I can express in words. My biggest thanks go to Roberta who continues to work with me to this day, to Ron who is deeply missed, and to their team that includes two of their sons David and Andy Squire.

Victoria Alexis Shearham is a graduate student currently studying in the Master of Education program at York University. In 2014, she graduated with top honors from York University, receiving her undergraduate degree in history, English, and concurrent education. Victoria is passionate about teaching, writing, and creating children's books. She says that she was excited to work on this project. Victoria screened video footage during the writing of this book and described scenes as she saw them. I am grateful to her for her hard work, her keen eye, and her gifts as a writer, illustrator and researcher.

Many graduate students in the Faculty of Education at York University transcribed material during the course of this study. I am grateful to all of them. Special thanks to Michelle Ali who worked on transcripts during the writing of this book.

I am grateful to Elma Thomas, York University Faculty of Education, who has helped with the transcription of data for this project from its earliest days. I am also grateful to York's Tara Somaroo, to Billy Chan, the York Faculty of Education IT genius, who keeps saving me from technological disaster, and to Graeme Howard and Jeffrey Zablotny who along with Victoria Shearham, have made the visual material in this book viable and visible.

I am deeply indebted to every member of the 1993-1996 Downtown Alternative School community—children, teachers, parents, staff, and administrators, all of whom contributed to this project. A special tribute to those who stayed with it over these many years. You are my heroes.

I wish to express my gratitude to the Social Sciences and Humanities Research Council of Canada (SSHRC) and the York University Faculty of Education, who have funded this study for more than twenty years. I also thank LaMarsh Centre at York University for support and contributions to this project during the early days.

High praise and thank you to Denny Taylor and the team at Garn Press for amazing work.

The drawings are by peacemakers from Bialik Hebrew Day School. The Peacemaker Program at Bialik Hebrew Day School is a peer mediation program where students in 5th grade help children from 1st – 5th grades work out their conflicts and help students find friends to play with at recess. This offers students leadership opportunities. A very special thanks to them and to their school counsellor, Debra Danilewitz who is also a Doctoral student at York University.

Katie's drawing of what peacemaking means to her

Special Thanks

To the following DAS student and parent contributors to this book:

Christine Ball; Dinny Biggs & Josh &Naomi &Abraham Blank; Jessica Brett-Caccia; Dale Brydon; Caitlin Burrell; Qwyn Charter; Hanna, Morgan, & Rick Edwards & Suzanne Jackson; Corey & Cathy Gulkin; Nathalie Herve-Azevedo; Savannah & Tarah Hoag; Nataleah Hunter-Young; Maya Limbertie; Alice Scott; Pandora Syperek; Sonia Taylor-Miglioni; Elli & Sharon Weisbaum; Molly & Anna Willats.

Nate's drawing of what peacemaking means to him

And to peacemaker-artists from Bialik Hebrew Day School and school counsellor Debra Danilewitz:

Gabby Dwosh, Natasha Enchin, Eric Ginzberg, Isabelle Goldman, Katie Hyman, Lena Kahn, Maya Krieger, Emily Lindzon, Sarah Mamelak, Nate Manis, Ryan Manis, Hannah Melnick, Jaime Polisuk, Maddie Taylor.

We loved all of your drawings. We regret we were only able to use a few of them.

Table of Contents

Praise for Raising Peacemakers

Raising Peacemakers shows that an authentic approach to managing child-to-child conflicts, learned in kindergarten, stayed with young children as they grew into adolescence and adulthood. It demonstrates by contrary example the profound error of standardized programs-in-a-box for "conflict resolution" and, by implication, much else in education. *Raising Peacemakers* accomplishes this by offering pieces of the rarest of educational research: a longitudinal study over 22 years—highly readable interlocking stories told by the same participants at different times of their lives. And holding these all together is the wise, quiet, honest voice of Esther Sokolov Fine. Read *Raising Peacemakers* as a meditation or as an inspiration. It is both.

Carole Edelsky
Professor Emerita
Arizona State University
February, 2015

Foreword

Esther Fine is interested still in providing alternatives for schools and teachers. *Raising Peacemakers* chronicles her work with the Downtown Alternative School and its peace curriculum. The school is an alternative to the bureaucratic organization of student bodies and minds; the curriculum is an alternative to the "war" pedagogy of learning as competition to be measured precisely in order to declare winners and losers. She presents these alternatives beautifully, telling stories to complement the already existing multi-modal and multi-genre texts that have documented the school and its peace curriculum across two decades. In the new telling, readers will see Esther's acts of love within the pedagogy of her lifetime.

This book also offers an alternative to what constitutes evidence in the evaluation of interventions. We live in a time with a growing emphasis on accountability, in which programs must prove their effectiveness through rigorous methods or be discontinued. Typically, that means an intervention becomes subject to experimental comparisons using the "gold standard" of cause and effect studies with random control trials. Survivors of that rigor earn the label "evidence based practice" and must be implemented with utmost fidelity within any relevant context. Accountability enthusiasts point toward medicine as the classic example of how rigor works to determine the most effective course for immediate action to solve any problem.

In *Raising Peacemakers*, Esther's practice based evidence demonstrates the limits of methods of evidence based practice in the real world. The lives of her students are too real, messy, complicated and changing, in ways that cannot be controlled or ignored in order to apply someone else's intervention with fidelity. Esther tells new stories that provide detailed evidence of how and why the peace curriculum changed the dynamic relationships among the school's children, adolescents and adults, both immediately and across time. Instead of settling for a single measurement of the question, "Did my intervention cause some learning?" she shows how adding peace to the curriculum altered the complex, personalized systems in the lives of the children before her. More than the immediate impact, Esther's stories let readers learn how "doing peace" made and sustained lasting, positive changes in students' lives. Medicine should be so accountable for its interventions.

Although situated in a different time and place, Esther's practice based evidence resonates with my understanding of the curriculum and pedagogy used at the Quaker school that "peacified" Kathleen's and my offspring during the1990s. Teachers Suzy, Eileen, Christy, Jane and Dan presented personal approaches to the principles of integrity, equality, community, simplicity, and peace. They took time to share their personalities, to know our kids, to expect that they could learn anything, and to take them seriously, but not too seriously. They forged lasting relationships built on the ideas that Laura and Tim Pat had to know themselves to love themselves, in order for them to have empathy for others both near and far. Our kids' embrace of self and other remains with them in their adult lives. Esther's report helped me to understand how and why two very different people are both at peace and make peace in a world that is not often peaceable.

The systematic compiling of Esther's research with the Downtown Alternative School community, the Quaker school our children attended, and other such stories, creates the practice based evidence to confront the evidence based practices that now control children's and teachers' lives in public schools.

Thank you Esther!

Patrick Willard Shannon
Professor of Education
Pennsylvania State University

February, 2015

Prologue

I believe there is a sixth sense. We are probably not born with it, but we are endowed with the potential to develop it. Under the right conditions, empathy and what I will call "ethical wisdom" can become central to a human child and grow along with that child to maturity. *Raising Peacemakers* is a story (really many stories) about how that can sometimes begin to happen.

Raising Peacemakers is a twenty-two year tale of kids growing up with peacemaking as a foundation. At Downtown Alternative School (DAS), a small public alternative elementary school in Toronto, Canada, children and adults explored peacemaking to help build a warm and inclusive community where ongoing conflicts and bullying behaviors could be faced and handled fairly and safely. This book presents an alternative approach to the public education of children in pre-K – 6th grades.

In this book, I look at the DAS peacemaking project, and how it took ordinary everyday child-to-child conflicts and viewed them as learning opportunities. It is my story and many stories, braided with interviews, transcripts, and my own experiences related as a narrative rather than an academic text. It is a trail of re-thinking, negotiating and re-negotiating, solving and re-solving (occasionally resolving) teaching and learning dilemmas. It is a tale of one school's optimistic effort to create and sustain healthy, safe, equitable, and academically relevant conditions for and with people whose lives were and are at stake in public education. It is about children and adults growing together as we work day by day to discover more about what it means (and what it takes) to become responsible citizens who care about each other, about our communities, and about the world.

Between their many inevitable conflicts, encouraged by teachers and parents, young children at Toronto's Downtown Alternative School (DAS) established their own ritual. They would double-cross their arms and clasp fingers in a group handshake to mark the conclusion of "a peacemaking." They would wipe away tears, giggle, move on to other things, or resume their play. They learned to express their viewpoints, listen, and include. The adults learned to hold back, hover, and accept what for the children constituted resolution, even when they (the adults) did not always fully get it. The DAS community was dedicated to the serious work, and to the joy of respectful relationships and power sharing. I invite you to step back more than twenty years, as I try to both explain how it all started and explore what has kept it alive to this day.

"Stay here and guard the body," commands Nataleah more than twenty years ago on the school playground. Nat is a participant in the *Children as Peacemakers* project that originated at Toronto's Downtown Alternative School. Nat and many others still help guard and guide the body of work that continues from this courageous journey of teachers, children and parents. What follows is *my* way to guard the body.

Esther Sokolov Fine

February, 2015

1

"Stay Here And Guard The Body"

"Stay here and guard the body," commands seven-year-old Nataleah on the playground, as she and her girlfriends conduct an ant funeral in a small circle during morning recess. Within a few sacred moments of spontaneous cooperative play, they dramatize essential rituals for the dead. While they didn't remain long at their funeral game, a surprising number of them have managed to stay connected with each other and with peacemaking.

DAS peacemakers: Tarah, Hanna and Qwyn

More than twenty years later, many of us are still guarding and forming new understandings about the body of work we have produced together. At times this feels like a miracle, but really it is a window on life-as-it-could-be for all students.

In the late 1980s, DAS made the most of its opportunity as a small public school in a busy downtown area. The school had an active parent community. It had devoted, talented and brave teachers, well-designed generous child-friendly space, abundant materials, and creative play equipment both indoors and outside in the schoolyard.

Teachers had more authority over their own practice in those days, and standardized testing was still several years in the future. So school was a place to create, question authority, debate issues of relevance, extend time frames, expand projects, and try out new ideas. The notion of peacemaking was introduced by the adults and taken up enthusiastically by the children. Behaviors began to alter as young voices rang out:

Do you want to solve this problem?

Do you want to solve it with us or the teachers?

Do you agree to listen?

No plugging your ears?

No interrupting?

No arguing back and forth?

No stepping on toes?

No denying?

This would be followed by intense discussion and then, "Is that all you have to say? Is the problem solved?" Crossed arms. A group handshake.

When we began the study *Children as Peacemakers* in 1993, we did not envision that it would follow students into adulthood and teachers into next schools, and eventually for some, into retirement. I had applied for and received a three-year grant to film at the school. I was awed by the realization that I would have sufficient funding to hire Roberta King and Ron Squire (very experienced in this field) as the filmmakers for this project.

For two whole years, at six-week intervals, we videotaped in classrooms. As well, we watched, listened and taped hallway and playground conversations among teachers, children and parents as they went about the business of school. We played hunches about where to focus our attention next as we tried to track (with crew, camera, and microphones) what seemed to us significant action and encounters. We looked for trouble and watched kids and teachers handle troubling moments. We also looked for examples of cooperative play and complex discussion.

After school, often until six o'clock, we taped interviews with parents, teachers and children. We asked students about moments we had seen and conversations we had overheard during the day. In the third year we videotaped follow-up interviews. I could not have predicted that many of the children would be so moved by their experiences at DAS and by our research project that they would still be coming back to study, talk, interview, and in some cases teach and write with us two decades later.

We began the research with three classrooms (approximately sixty children, some as young as four) and three teachers: Ann Lacey, Lori McCubbin, and Marie Lardino. The whole community opted in and signed consent forms. To this day, with repeated funding from the Social Sciences and Humanities Research Council of Canada and from the Faculty of Education at York University,

Roberta King and I have continued to periodically interview teachers, parents, and especially students (some of whom are now teachers) from that 1993 community, to learn about their developing ideas and experiences in and beyond school.

When I joined the DAS staff in 1987, I job-shared with Ann Lacey in the junior/senior kindergarten and also worked closely with other teachers including Joan Baer. Joan taught the first group of DAS peacemakers, the 2nd – 3rd grade pioneers, who really got this project off the ground. Our work became well known in Ontario and other parts of Canada, and in 1991 Ann was sent by the Toronto Board of Education (now the TDSB—Toronto District School Board) to be a peacemaking coach/ambassador in eleven larger elementary schools. At the same time I was hired to teach in the Faculty of Education at York University. Several outstanding new teachers were hired at DAS. Soon after, Joan Baer retired. Ann returned to DAS following two years of sharing her knowledge with other schools, and I remained at York with a plan to focus my research on the DAS peacemaking work. DAS was moved to a spacious and beautiful location farther downtown, where it would draw many of its students from a more diverse residential community that included apartments, townhouses, and co-op housing. It would also welcome students from outside the school district on a first-come-first-served basis. There was a waiting list for the out of district children. Finally, there was enough space to expand from K-3. DAS would now go up to 6th grade.

Early peacemaking efforts at DAS were about teachers, children and parents working together to produce what they saw as ethical high-quality schooling experiences. They were coming to terms, questioning, rethinking, and sometimes changing the terms. They were daring to cross challenging boundaries, to consider social and pedagogical problems, and to try, when possible, to solve them. Teachers and children were growing together as they worked to discover more about what it means (and what it takes) to become responsible citizens who care about each other, about their own community, and about the world. We continued to film and interview as the children grew. From the early days there, our research has followed the people, rather than the school itself.

2

Nataleah

"Stay here and guard the body." The voice of Nataleah, star of the ant funeral, still echoes in my head. A seemingly thoughtful and confident seven-year-old, Nataleah was one of several African Canadian children at DAS. In 1995 the DAS population was still predominantly white, middle-class, and English speaking.

The ant funeral: "Stay here and guard the body."

Nataleah is on the playground. It is morning recess. She and a group of friends, all girls ranging in age from five to nine, have seated themselves in a circle on the ground surrounding a small mound of sand upon which they are heaping more sand and performing their version of a funeral. It is an ant burial. "A moment of silence please," says Nat in her strong authoritative voice. "Starting now," says her friend Savannah.

Victoria Shearham (graduate assistant) describes the video footage of this funeral as follows:

> A group of children gather in a small circle and kneel in the sand. Nataleah is crouching down. Some of the children begin to toss the pebbles into the center of the circle, while Nataleah says, "James, James stepped on an ant—well, um, a queen ant, and we buried it."
>
> A child in the circle shouts, "Moment of silence!" The talking amongst the children continues.
>
> Nataleah, holding a pretend tape player, quickly calls out, "A moment of silence for the …"
>
> The other children continue talking. One girl announces, "Hold it! I must be the …"
>
> The girl struggles to find the term for her role, "I'm the church, um, the church … the judge."
>
> A child comes up to the group and inquires, "What are you guys doing?" Multiple children in the circle begin to reply, and the girl at Nataleah's right cries out that they are trying to have a funeral for a bug. Nataleah adjusts her headphones and replies, "A moment of silence, please!" One of the children mimics her request. "A moment of silence." Nataleah repeats, "Moment of silence."
>
> The children now lean into the center of the circle. Nataleah holds her hands to her face and uses her tape player to cover her eyes. She looks up, adjusts her headphones, and repeats

her request for a moment of silence, and the children chime into the end of the sentence. They call out in unison for "silence."

The girl to Nataleah's left (Savannah) announces, "Starting now!" The children remain silent. A couple of the girls hold their hands together as if in prayer. Nataleah, eyes closed, has her hands clasped around her tape player in the same manner, resting her elbows on her knees. She opens her eyes for a second to shush the person opposite her.

As soon as the "moment" is over the children begin to talk, some standing, some kneeling, when one girl suggests that they say, "Two things about it." The girl continues, "You are beautiful, and um, what is it?"

Nataleah, who is picking up and dropping pebbles, says, "You are beautiful, but you died."

The other girls follow her lead and offer a few words about the ant, "You are nice, but someone killed you."

"You were beautiful and …"

The girl to Nataleah's right begins to toss pebbles into the center of the circle and chimes in, "You had the colors of a flower, but …"

Another child picks up on this and says, "Who's got a flower for the funeral?"

"Not me," another girl answers.

The children begin to chatter, when one girl says, "Come on, let's go and find one!"

The group starts to separate. Nataleah stands. The girl to her right stays kneeling and announces that she will, "stay here."

Nataleah, holding the tape player to her ear, uses her right hand to emphatically point to the center of the circle, while she exclaims, "Stay here and guard the body!"

“Ok,” one of the children replies. Nataleah turns to leave. The bell rings.

“Oh man, we have to go,” Nataleah says, as she turns a knob on her tape player. The headphones slip down over her face again. Nataleah stoops while she and the other girls, who are still sitting in the circle, scoop handfuls of pebbles onto the mound. With each toss, Nataleah repeats (presumably to the ant), “Goodbye, goodbye, goodbye.”

The other children follow, and some echo Nataleah’s word, “goodbye.” One girl says, “Hope you go to animal heaven.”

Another voice, “No, go to, go to animal heaven.”

Some of the children continue to toss pebbles. One girl cautions, “Nobody step on this!”

Nataleah, now standing above the circle exclaims, “The devil! Go to the devil! You were … Christine. Go to the devil!” Nataleah then alters her tone and says, “Go to God!” She follows this with a chuckle.

Another child announces, “We have to leave.”

The circle begins to break up, but many of the participants, including Nataleah, are still huddled. Four of the children are now standing and watching. One girl says, “Somebody might step on it.”

Nataleah, standing up and facing the burial mound, holds out her right hand and says dramatically, “Goodbye. Goodbye, my …”

Her voice starts to trail off as she begins to tip over, just catching her balance. The bell rings again. Nataleah clasps her headphones to her ears and says dramatically, “Goodbye, goodbye, goodbye.”

One girl says, “Let it suffer in peace.”

Another girl adds, “Ya, let it be at peace.”

> As Nataleah turns to walk toward the school entrance, the others follow her, except for Tabitha, the youngest. Tabitha lingers for a moment, caresses the burial ground, and a split second later pops up, plants both feet on the grave, and scampers toward the school entrance.

During much of this scene that Victoria describes, Nat has been in charge, the strongest voice in a small group of friends on this particular morning. These girls, like many children their age, are playing at life and death and ritual, forming their own social order and a narrative. Nat has been particularly concerned with the corpse. Pretend or otherwise, a dead ant has held center stage. While we filmed a wide range of play, controversy, and problem solving, none was as replete with ceremony as the ant funeral, and none as overtly concerned with life and death.

As an adult, Nataleah reflects on her experiences at DAS. She ponders an experience she had one afternoon in 1995 when she was seven. It was an afternoon of self-portraits in the art room, a scene we filmed in which children created outlines of each other on butcher paper.

The DAS art room: "Be good to yourself."

In the scene, they trace around each other's bodies and then use scissors to create life-size cutouts. They paint their faces, their arms, their legs, their hair, and their clothing, using brushes with skill and focus. Nat is one of two dark-skinned children in the art room at that time. A student teacher of Middle Eastern descent, Zamira, works with Nat. Zamira's response to Nat shows that she understands how it feels to be "other." Nat appears to be painting joyfully, even as she complains about being "made" to do this. As she examines her nearly finished work, she chats to herself, aware of her classmates who are also painting. Nat says to her friend Christine, "If you were me, you would be ugly." She laughs as she says this. No child is ugly, but Nat is a particularly beautiful child. Zamira does not let her remark pass without response. "Be good to yourself," she says.

Victoria Shearham describes the video footage of this classroom interaction as follows:

> Kneeling on the floor above her nearly finished portrait, Nataleah proclaims, "We're all just a bunch of people who don't look like our pictures."
>
> She moves her hand up and down emphatically.
>
> Zamira interjects, reminding her, "They're an impression."
>
> Unfazed, Nataleah continues her original train of thought, "Ever noticed that?" She shakes her head emphasizing her point.
>
> Zamira, attempting again to persuade Nataleah that the portraits do not have to look like a mirror image, repeats, "Nataleah, they're impressions. You have to remember, they're just an impression of what you look like."

Nataleah looks down at her picture and, with strong emotion, points to her portrait and raises her shoulders. "This isn't an impression," she declares, dramatically lifting her head to look up. Moving her left hand up and down like a skilled orator, Nataleah proclaims, "Whoever made this be … whoever made me do this is going to be real sorry!" She smiles quizzically.

Attempting to calm the unnerved Nataleah, Zamira says, "I think you did a great job."

Not satisfied with the comment, Nataleah continues her performance. She briefly raises her hand to her head before flinging it down and looking up at the ceiling while she cries, "An impression of me, ha!" Nataleah rolls her eyes.

Nataleah commences work on the eyes of her portrait—the windows to the soul in artwork. Turning to the other girls who are painting behind her, Nataleah calls out, "Your eyes always look the same!"

Someone didn't quite catch the comment, "What?"

Nataleah, shifting her position, repeats her artistic commentary, "Your eyes always look the same."

"Mine?" A girl questions, picking up on the comment.

"Ya, yours!" Nataleah replies as she commences work on the nose of her portrait. In order to follow up on the comment, Nataleah says, "You should come see *my* eyes." She leans back to observe her fellow artists, "I look like a cat!" The comment is followed by giggles.

Zamira, sitting across the room now answers Nataleah with an "ok" signal.

The girl next to Zamira replies to the comment differently. While continuing to paint her shoes green instead of white she calls, "Do my shoes look the same? I don't think so!" Another girl looks down at her own shoes while she dunks her paintbrush in a water bucket and looks up smiling.

Nataleah, continuing her portrait, stops to look back at the other artists and announces, "Christine, if you were me you would look ugly!" Nataleah giggles. She pauses briefly, looking at the girls behind her, as if waiting for a reply that does not come. She turns back to her work, encouraged by Zamira who reminds her, "Be good to yourself."

Nataleah appears to have lost one shoe and sock during the painting process. She takes some yellow paint and carefully tiptoes over the portraits to return to her own masterpiece. Leaning over her painting again, Nataleah engages in conversation, "Yaaa, I asked you …"

The girl, off camera, cuts in, "No actually …"

Nataleah speaks over her, "And you said no."

The other girl, unshaken by the comment, continues, "And you said no. No I'm not helping you. You said I, I can't help you. Go away, I don't want to …"

Nataleah uses her paintbrush as a pointer, "*She* said that!"

Nataleah declares, "I have to go get some black paint," and quickly turns to the girl across from her, "Look at my head!" Nataleah's lips curl into a smile as she points to her portrait and laughs.

Nataleah resumes painting her shoe while Zamira gives a heads-up, "Ok, you have another ten minutes. I'm giving you a ten-minute warning and then we're going to go outside," she says before replying to an artistic question, "Ok, you can paint all your fingernails, but you have ten minutes."

Nataleah quickly stands up. "I have to paint my fingernails," she remembers and begins to walk across her portrait. Zamira watches closely and appears to hold her breath while Nataleah carefully steps on the page with her bare foot, before gently planting her shoe on the paper and then making a final step over the artwork. "And my shoelace," Nataleah adds to her list of things to do.

Likely influenced by the girl behind her who is painting red cheeks on her portrait, Nataleah travels back to her own portrait declaring, "All I have to do is my cheeks!" Skillfully, Nataleah bobs over her portrait to paint a small, pinkish circle on the cheeks, whispering, "I don't look like this." Nataleah stands up and makes an elaborate, full body stretch before spinning around and starting to walk away.

Nataleah

> A girl stands next to Nataleah and says, with resignation, "That's what I look like." The girl then looks towards Nataleah and asks, "[do you] like mine?"
>
> Nataleah appears not to hear her and instead redirects the attention back to her own piece. "I do not look like that!" she declares, pointing to her painting and walks away. The other girl turns to view the portrait but remains silent.

Now, all these years later, reading Victoria's description, Nat's words still puzzle me; they puzzle the adult Nataleah as well. In 2013, Nataleah phones Roberta King to see if she can get a copy of the documentary for her parents as a gift before she leaves for a short-term job as a social worker in Jamaica. Of course she can have a copy. And of course, we schedule an interview with her. During the interview Nat tears up when she talks about her self-portrait. She is unsure about her use of the word ugly and what it means about the school, about her friends, about herself, and her history.

It's Summer 2014, and Nat is back home in Toronto. She has spent much of the past year working in the University of Toronto's Anti-Racism & Cultural Diversity Office (ARCDO). I invite her to have dinner with me to discuss the next phase of the peacemaking project and the book I am writing, this book. We email back and forth and decide to meet at The Boulevard Café, where we can eat outdoors and have a leisurely conversation. I am hoping she will give me a go-ahead nod. I want to be sure she is comfortable with what I am writing.

We eat, we talk, we plan and strategize; I give her my twenty-five page book proposal. I am doing the smart thing, the right thing, the risky thing, taking a chance that she might be disturbed by my portrayal of her. Nat promises to email her response. I am nervous about this. What if she is offended? What if she doesn't give me that nod of approval, or what if she doesn't want to contribute to this? Then what? The ethics questions matter not just because of accuracy, not just because of privacy rights and the law, but also because of mutual respect and human decency. After all, part of the discussion is about her beauty and what the word "ugly" meant to her seven-year-old self. My hope is that Nat and I are good enough peacemakers that if differences do arise, we will be able to negotiate our way through them.

I will learn as I go. In a way this is a next step in the research. In August I receive her nod and some rich answers to the questions I have asked Nat. She writes to me as follows:

> **Esther:** "Did we set kids up for difficulty? If so, was it worth it?"
>
> **Nat:** The short answer is, "Yes and yes." The long answer is, "Yes, and well … it depends." I gather, only based on my interactions with some "non-DAS kids," that DAS was a very unique environment with some very remarkable teachers, parents, and children. The way I felt at DAS—and my mom would be the first to agree—could only be described as "loved." The teachers were more than just teachers, and the other kids in my class, many of whose names I still remember, were more than just my classmates. That made DAS more than just my school.
>
> DAS socialized me in a way that was so organic, honest and authentic that I found the follow-up school environments confusing and often hurtful …
>
> "Why do I have to call you 'Miss'?"
>
> "What do you mean I have to walk on the right side of the hallway?"
>
> "Oh, you mean you don't care much for my point of view or my sense of humor?"

"My questions, if not directly concerning whatever we are being taught, are irrelevant? I see."

DAS taught me to question everything; that there was never just "one side." Most important, I learned that my feelings were truths. MY truths. And that if we each had truths then there was no "right way," there was only ever the way that worked best for you, at that time, in that moment.

It wasn't until Esther approached me to participate in the follow-up documentary [study] that I actually noticed the links between how DAS teachers taught children to resolve problems and how I still aim to resolve problems today. My approach to conflict as an adult (full disclosure, most of the time) has a lot of similarities to the DAS peacemaking principles, but it's hard to apply them when the other parties aren't playing with the same rulebook. After narrowly escaping an adolescence filled with second-guessing, low self-confidence, and hesitancy, I finally feel like I've made a return to those principles with a renewed respect for myself, my perspectives, and the perspectives of others.

When your teacher is your best friend, you believe everything that he or she tells you. You trust them when they commend you and when they encourage you to do better. Leaving DAS meant leaving the comfort of that trust, forced to heed the advice of adults and other children who seemingly had little stake in my well-being. A hard pill to swallow for any nine-year-old, but an inevitable and necessary lesson. Life isn't easy.

The documentary — *Life at School: The D.A.S. Tapes* — reacquainted me with a much younger and much more confident version of myself. My friends found my outspoken and animated (dramatic) persona hilarious. I watched the scenes I was in over and over trying to figure out where I learned those leadership skills and when/why they went dormant.

Though the ant burial was an Oscar-worthy performance,

the self-portrait scene left the strongest mark. Who knows what seven-year-old Nat was thinking when she was poking fun at her painting. Was it wise commentary on our social standards of beauty? Was I trying to make others feel better about their portraits by making fun of my own? Or, was I just playing it up for the cameras?

"Christine, if you were me, you'd be ugly." Such a conclusive statement from a seven-year-old, pronounced as fact.

When all of us were brought together to watch the premiere screening of the doc years later, I didn't know what I meant by that statement then, and I don't know now. Be it a comment about my true physical nature, or the portrait I was drawing, I think the message was that Christine's appearance held more weight than mine, and that she need not worry.

Here is the bio I asked Nataleah to write:

I was born in Toronto to a Jamaican father and Guyanese (raised British) mother who were both very "community minded" and political in nature. I have two older brothers (+8 years, +12 years) and an older sister (+10 years). I started kindergarten by attending Alpha [Alternative School] but my parents only did that so that once a spot opened up at DAS I could switch. I believe I attended DAS from SK to grade 3, leaving DAS for Orde Street Public School in grade 4 because my mother wanted me to start French immersion. I did grades 7 & 8 at King Edward Public School and grades 9 to 12 at Harbord Collegiate Institute.

I completed my undergraduate education at McMaster University in 2009 with a Bachelor of Social Work and a BA in Sociology (which I only completed concurrently because I had to in order to enroll in McMaster's Social Work Program; in retrospect, I should've chosen something like creative writing or journalism).

I first developed the intention to go into Social Work when I began attending the St. Stephen's Community House Youth Drop in Centre (then called "the Arcade") in about the 8th grade and continued throughout High School. It amazed me that someone's profession was working with youth in what seemed like such a fun environment. I was hooked. Attending the Arcade also exposed me to many of the realities facing young black men in low-income communities, the over-policing and racial profiling being the most stark of those realities. Hearing my peers talk about being stalked and beaten by police officers ignited an interest into "justice" systems and how they could be so brazenly unjust.

My third year undergraduate practicum was at the Hamilton-Wentworth Detention Centre in the Youth Unit. This was a maximum-security facility where they sent all of the young men from Toronto who were either being detained (awaiting trial or sentencing) or completing the secure (as in "jailed") portion of their sentence. My fourth year practicum took place in the Access & Equity Office in the City of Hamilton. This was very policy oriented, which I wasn't used to (or very into), but is ironically relatively close to what I'm doing now. It's funny how things come full-circle.

After undergrad I spent a month in Burkina Faso with Global Youth Network. I left for Burkina with such excitement as I embarked on what I had framed as a sort of "rites of passage" first trip to Africa. However, I came back very discouraged about international development work and a little disappointed in my own naiveté. I met incredible people while in Burkina, but I think I was ill prepared for the confronting I would inevitably do with my own privilege and power.

Over the next two years, before I started grad school, I worked in a number of youth serving positions with a variety of organizations, beginning with Central Toronto Probation in the Provincial Government's summer experience program. I then moved to Terry Fox House (Operation Springboard); an open-custody facility in downtown Toronto. They were a

7 or 8 bed facility made up of all male youth who were either being detained or completing the open custody portion of their sentence.

I lasted there full-time for nine months (it was only after two months that I began searching for another job), and then I moved to part-time/casual where I could nurse my burnout a little more gracefully. My move to part-time coincided with the beginning of my position at Leave Out Violence (LOVE) Ontario—a youth violence prevention organization that uses media arts programming to promote anti-violence with young people. I was there for about 14 months before beginning my graduate studies.

I received my MSW from Ryerson University and loved every moment of it. The Ryerson School of Social Work has some of the most amazing professors and presents their students with great opportunities, one of which led me to a graduate assistantship with Stephan Lewis who was teaching a course on the United Nations Millennium Development Goals as a distinguished visiting professor in residence. Having the good fortune of listening to one of the world's greatest speakers on a weekly basis for four months led me right back into the world of international development following graduation. My MSW research project looked at community murals as an effective tool for youth community reintegration (returning to community from criminal custody). I looked at community murals in the San Romanoway (Jane/Finch) community.

Towards the end of my MSW, in 2012, I began applying for overseas placements and eventually landed one in Montego Bay, Jamaica with CUSO International. I was placed with the Social Development Commission in St. James as a Youth Community Mobilization Officer, working with youth clubs in and around Montego Bay. Yet another great experience, where I inevitably learned more about myself than I did anything else, but I developed a true love for the island and its people (my people).

My return to Toronto was sparked by a job offer at the University of Toronto's Anti-Racism & Cultural Diversity Office (ARCDO), where I currently work. The ARCDO has bridged my love of youth work with my love of anti-racist work in an interesting way. I'm enjoying the experience, though it's by no means easy; I feel like this experience is preparing me for something great.

Here is an excerpt from our filmed interview with Nat (summer 2013):

Question: Do you remember any race issues at DAS?

Nat: Yah I do. I do remember race issues at DAS. There was ahhhh. [*chuckles*] And I guess I don't know that as a child I would have signaled this as a race issue, but there was a little play structure we had in one of the classrooms, a little house or something, that we could all go inside. And I was in there with a couple of other students, one of whom had all of these hair things, these hair barrettes and scrunchies and something. So there was something she had that maybe would go on top of … like a bun. You put your hair in a bun and then [*clamps hands together to show how it would go on top of a bun*], and I think I picked it up and I was going to put it on and she was like, "Oh no that's only for someone with long hair." And I was … kind of confused [*laughs*] I was like, "Well, no, I can wear this, I can put my hair in a pony tail and put it on." I do remember that, the situation and understanding that *she* didn't understand that I could use the hair thing as well. But, that would be, kind of, that's the only thing that comes to mind really. There were other black students at DAS who I remember, and I don't ever remember feeling like the odd one out or something like that at DAS. But there's always that stuff when you're dealing with children. That they just don't … children form their own conclusions about things. I'm sure that there were other little things that children talk about but nothing overarching or major.

Question: When you watch the film now as an adult, do you see race issues that you wouldn't have seen as a child?

Nat: When I watch the film now as an adult, the one thing that really sticks out to me is the self-portrait that I did of myself. [*Begins to cry*] I wonder if … cuz I've tried to think about that comment that I made and I wonder if that was a reflection of how I saw myself, and I think it probably was. I don't know if that had a … I don't think … but I definitely didn't think that I was attractive or something. [*chuckles*] I didn't know what I thought. I don't know what [*age*] I was … 7 or 8 or something like that. I don't know what 8-year-olds think about or want to be like or whatever. But I think [*chuckles*] my reaction to feeling unhappy with the way I was, was to make a joke about it. I was trying to make Christine feel better with the comment that I made, I think, that was my intention I think [*chuckles*] … I think it was Christine I was talking to. And you know, I said, "If you were me, you would be ugly," which doesn't make any sense. But I think I was trying to tell her that there was nothing wrong with her picture or that, "Look at my picture, mine is worse." You know, I don't know what that was a response to but … [*here Nat is in tears*]

Nat: I'm not sure what triggered my search for the DAS documentary. It may have been a comment that my dad made. My dad has made comments kind of throughout the years, "You know we never got a copy of that documentary. Or we never did …"

I know they always had it in the back of their mind. I've always had it in the back of my mind too. I definitely remember the screening and being totally kind of shocked at how loud I was [*laughs*]. But I don't know what it was about that time … I kinda wanted to see it too and so I started Googling.

Question: This is a question I've been wanting to ask somebody for many years. Was there really a dead ant?

Nat: [*Laughs*]

Question: A dead ant in the ant funeral.

Nat: You know what? I think there was a dead ant, because there were so many of us gathered around that. We wouldn't have done that if, for nothing, you know. That was the type of thing that we did at recess was find something to make a big story about. [*chuckles*] Create some spectacle. [*laughs*] It's so ridiculous, but that's what we [were] like. You let your imagination run away with you. One thing leads to another, and then before you know it you're having a funeral for an ant. [*laughs*]

Question: When you watch that as the opening scene of the film, what do you think about?

Nat: The first thing that comes to mind [*laughs*] is, "This is ridiculous," when I watch that opening scene, I think, "This is ridiculous, but in a funny way." Kids, just being kids. But I also … this is the natural process, this is what we do. You know, when something dies, we have a funeral for it and like, you know, bury it, that's what you do. I remember being on a field trip, I think, with Ann Lacey and I think we went to her house on the Island … Ann had always had rats that she brought to school. She had pet rats, and I think one of them had died, and I think one of them may have been in her freezer … I think we buried it. It's what we did, you know we had funerals for dead animals. So, I think I look at that and think this is hilarious, but we cared about this dead ant enough to have a funeral and, you know, we had to say some words for the dead ant and … yah, I don't know, I don't know. What was I saying? "A moment of silence." We knew that we needed to have … I don't know … I have no idea what I was thinking. I just know, like, that when someone dies, you do all of these things. In what order, who knows. Clearly, we had been influenced in some way in regard to that.

All these years later, it is a huge gift to be able to consult with

Nataleah on these matters. Her speculations, questions, and insights challenge, confirm and clarify in ways I trust.

3

Flashback To Kindergarten 1988: The Year Before Peacemaking

Esther Sokolov Fine (2003). "Storytime," *Talking Points*

The DAS kindergarten day ends with story time. It's winter 1988, late afternoon. I am at DAS with Linda, our kindergarten assistant, in one of Toronto's first all day junior/senior kindergartens. Ann Lacey has gone home for the day. Now *I'm* in the straight-back chair, at the front of the room. The chair is made of blond wood with high-gloss varnish that has been rubbed away in key spots, marking the teacher's place. Behind me is an upright piano with the open songbook handed down to Ann and me by my mother. In front of me are twenty-three children in scraggly jeans, falling-off socks, and paint-spattered shirts. Some have thumbs in their mouths. Others caress small lumps of yellow and blue striped play-dough, turning it over and over in their hands, eyes drooping. A few cling to soggy remnants of baby blankets, mere strings. Several are not yet four, while the oldest are already six. Tuna flakes and banana stick to the carpet and to the bottoms of little socks. Scent of childhood fills the air.

Arnie Barker is five. His chair, the tiny kindergarten variety, is also made of blond wood with high-gloss varnish. Arnie has positioned himself just off the carpet, at the far wall facing me. He tips his chair backwards on its hind legs, as far as it can go without falling. He knows how to do this perfectly. The mocking gleam in his half-closed eyes tells me that he has practiced.

Just behind him are the cubbies, baby lockers where children hang coats on low hooks and stash secret candy bars, stuffed animals, drawings for parents, and red crayons. Little kids can be clever at getting exactly what they want.

When I was a child, I was more concerned with what others wanted from me. My Gramma Tillie wanted me to be a kindergarten teacher. "A woman," she said, "must have a trade or a profession." In the early 1900's, at age sixteen, Gramma Tillie had immigrated along with many other Russian Jews, first to England and then to the United States. In her early teens she had been trained as a seamstress.

"You'll grow up to be a kindergarten teacher just like your mother," she informed me.

"Never," I insisted.

"Someday you'll write my story," she often said. "One child has to; I think it will be you."

"Maybe," I said.

My father wanted me to win spelling bees like his nephew, grapple with the physics experiments he constructed in the basement, eat soft-boiled eggs, punch child assailants in the nose, and play with a toy gun. My mother wanted me to be a truth teller and a pianist. She wanted me to fatten up and grow taller than she was. My cousins wanted me to repeat swear words and get my clothes dirty. Pressure from all sides built and built until sometimes I just went off like a bomb. Lots of things could set me off. My snow pants, for example, could set me off just as it was time to leave for school. My father could set me off. He had the knack, especially at the dinner table. Now, years later, it turns out that Arnie Barker can set me off. He sits at the back of the kindergarten smirking, rocking his chair back and forth, teetering on the edge of an emotional cliff.

"Arnie, please sit up."

"Why?" he asks.

"Because it's story time," I answer. "Please sit on the carpet with the other kids. You're going to fall."

"Make me," he says, as another child moves his chair to the back.

"Make us," they chant in unison, rocking back and forth, smiling in that special way known only to an experienced Nemesis.

Arnie Barker is my father at five, the bad boy who knows how to fight. My father is dead, recently dead, and I have to take charge. I can't blow. There's too much at stake now and too many children waiting for the ending. I leap to my feet, spring to the back of the room, pluck Arnie Barker from his chair, fly through the doorway and up one flight of stairs to Joan's 3rd grade classroom.

I make a panther's entrance, slow, silent, intense.

"Joan," I say, as the 3rd graders pause. "It's time for Arnie Barker to be with older children."

"Leave him with us," Joan says, putting a warm arm around his shoulders and drawing him into the room. "Find a spot at the writing table, Arnie. The other kids will get your notebook and pencil."

I return to my chair. The children are waiting quietly. The boy who was sitting with Arnie has moved back to the carpet. Others lie on the floor; two have fallen asleep. Breathing more easily, I finish our story, loving this small alternative school, where teachers rely on each other and no one has to go over the edge. Arnie Barker is in the arms of older children. We are all safe for the moment, but there is a great deal more to learn.

At dismissal time, I climb the stairs to reclaim Arnie Barker. I peer through the doorway. Older children are helping him pack up his drawings. I extend my hand and say, “It’s home time now, let’s go downstairs and get your coat and boots.”

Arnie accepts my hand. Together we descend the stairs. “It’s not fair,” he says. “Teachers always get to decide what time it is.”

4

Ann Lacey Looks Back

Ann Lacey knows how to connect with children. In a ten-years-later interview (2005) she reminisces about her years at DAS and talks about humor, how surprisingly funny the children could be, and how she herself continued to be able to be surprised by them. She talks about the importance of being able to "develop things with children by being present with them in the moment and responding to their questions, their interests, and their curiosity." She views herself as helping children catch on to things, continuing to follow through as they explore and try to understand something more clearly. Ann tells us that often she could "do it on the spot," that she used her intuition a lot in teaching kindergarten. She didn't follow a script. She was herself, real, connected; the children responded to her and trusted her.

Ann talks about the starting moments in the late 1980s when DAS peacemaking was just emerging. A big "turning point" she tells us, was talking together with parents out on the playground, watching the children, watching the problems that occurred in a repetitive way, and seeing the same children come back to the adults day after day with the same problems, not learning how to figure them out. Ann gives examples of repeated complaints, "So and so took my ball," and "So and so took the swing from me … so we began to kind of look around for another way to handle it."

Ann remembers a general dissatisfaction with the way the conflicts were being handled. She saw that teachers "were always in charge of deciding what would happen in the problem and giving out consequences." She says, "We were just looking for something else … there was a group called Parents for Peace. And they [some of the DAS parents] had seen a video of children solving problems in a schoolyard in inner city San Francisco …" Ann recalls details about the video clip … the *Conflict Managers* approach (Sadalla et al., 1990) where certain children who had been "trained" to solve problems, went out with clipboards and armbands to "solve" problems and write down details of what was happening.

Ann goes on to explain that once this had caught on at DAS, kindergarten children began to fold peacemaking into their play. She talks about seeing this especially in the blocks and drama centers of the classroom:

> Esther and I had noticed that they were playing at peacemaking, and then we began to really think they could … why couldn't they learn [this]? If they could play it, they could learn how to do it … that was kind of revolutionary, I think, to look at young children that way and to think that they might be able to take on some of their own problems. They discarded all those props very quickly. They liked the shape of the session, that it had rules, and that you ask people how they feel, and then you listen … they liked that part, so they kept that shape a little bit.

We began to notice that peacemaking questions (the rules) were different every time. Ann continues:

> No fiddling … and then you would know, oh that's that kid who always fiddles and you can't get him to talk because he's

> fiddling. So ... the rules began to be customized to the different situations, but the spirit of it was always talking it out until you felt better, and the concept of reconciliation was very strong from the beginning ... we began to notice after a while that what *resolved* meant to them was sometimes different [from] what it meant to us ... and then we had to respect what they needed from it; that they get what they needed from it, not that we get what we needed ... they would sometimes get back to playing and we wouldn't think it was solved yet, but they obviously felt better enough to play.

As teachers, we were accustomed to a different style of problem solving and to maintaining control. We had to learn to hold back and allow the play to resume. We began to understand that intervening when the children had "made their peace," could be more of an interference than a help.

5

Epiphany on Queen Street

It's 1988. We teachers are hurrying back to school after a hasty but delicious dim sum lunch. We love the dumplings and the spring rolls. We use chopsticks and share the food. Now we are in a rush, so we do not go to the corner to cross at the lights. There's almost no traffic. There are five of us. Idealists. Teachers who want to make our little school good, better—best is not the issue because we de-emphasize competition. Just as we are about to J-walk, we spot a small corner store, a "convenience store."

"Let's buy a Lottery ticket," shouts out someone from our group. So even though this will make us a minute or two later than we already are, we can't resist. Linda and Judy will cover for us. They are already in the classrooms. They always cover for us, and they probably can't afford the dim sum lunch they insist they don't really want and would never allow us to pay for.

I was raised by a father who did not believe in organized religion or gambling, but he has died recently and I think, what the hell, certain we will win at some things but probably not at this. This is my first ever Lottery ticket. With a small twinge of guilt, I hand over my dollar. I'm in. Then begins the J-walk. I am a little behind the rest of them. I am always a bit behind. I'm having a flash, an insight, a spark, an epiphany.

I am job-sharing with Ann Lacey, working "part-time" (though I have due respect for the maxim, teaching can never truly be "part-time") so that I can complete my doctoral dissertation on "outsider kids" in a public housing project community. I'm doing too many things at once, and my head is spinning with ideas and new experiences.

We are hopeful, teaming with exhilaration and a sense of purpose. I think of my dissertation as separate from my work at DAS because the data were gathered at another school in my own classroom several years earlier. Then in a flash, in the middle of Queen Street, J-walking slightly behind the other teachers and a bit late getting back from lunch hour dim sum, there and then, it is ALL about peacemaking. Everything is about peacemaking. Everything connects. I try to explain this to Ann, but she is walking ahead of me and watching for cars.

"It all connects," I call out.

"What did you say?" shouts Ann.

"Everything connects. My dissertation. Peacemaking. Team teaching. It's all the same."

"Right," says Ann, who already understands such things in her own brilliantly organic way. "Of course it does. Let's talk later, Esther. Hurry."

For me this is an epiphany. For Ann it is obvious. I'm always walking a bit behind but often busy thinking ahead. If it connects to my kind of research, then it's something we will be able to document, analyze together, and share in a formal way. I think back to day one of the peacemaking. It went something like this:

Downtown Alternative School was seriously exploring conflict resolution approaches that had been tried elsewhere with some hints of success. None was found for kindergarten or primary age children, but a promising one called "Conflict Managers," intended for somewhat older children, was being tried by the Community Board in San Francisco. (Sadalla et al., 1990)

DAS teacher Joan Baer introduced some of the San Francisco ideas to her 2nd – 3rd grade class—"the big kids." She positioned the children in a circle on the carpet to watch a clip from a San Francisco news item and then invited them to engage in a group discussion. While Joan's students found the Conflict Managers concept intriguing, there were a few things they wished to do differently. They wanted a different name, so they made suggestions, voted, and named it "peacemakers." They decided that the four 3rd graders would act as the first DAS peacemakers. They told us the armbands they saw in the video made kids look like police, but they made paper ones just to see how it would feel to have those bands of authority on their bodies. They wanted to try it straight away and then have another meeting to discuss how it went.

The children rushed back from recess, out of breath with enthusiasm. They dropped the paper armbands in the recycle bin and settled upon another fundamental change. Instead of having designated peacemakers, they wanted that role to be open to any and all of the kids in the school. Each child, any age, any grade, could decide if and when he or she was ready to be a peacemaker. When that time came the child would declare herself or himself to be a peacemaker, and that would be that.

A larger meeting was held next morning with the whole school, all staff and all kids. Everyone gathered in the hallway just outside the makeshift library. The 2nd – 3rd grade children improvised a couple of skits to demonstrate peacemaking. The others seemed to get it, like it, feel it, and want it. They did it all day everywhere, inside the school and on the playground. Some did it sitting together on the rim of a car tire near the school steps.

Kids can tell when something feels right. Sometimes there is a lot of crying during a peacemaking. Always a teacher hovers and, when necessary, guides the conversation and sometimes takes over. Peacemaking is an intense and serious social undertaking, huge in fact. There was much to learn. A few teachers from Toronto travelled to Washington D.C. to attend seminars with trainers from San Francisco. They came back charged with energy and enthusiasm for this new approach. They brought it to the children, who adapted it in innovative ways.

The Peaceosaurus

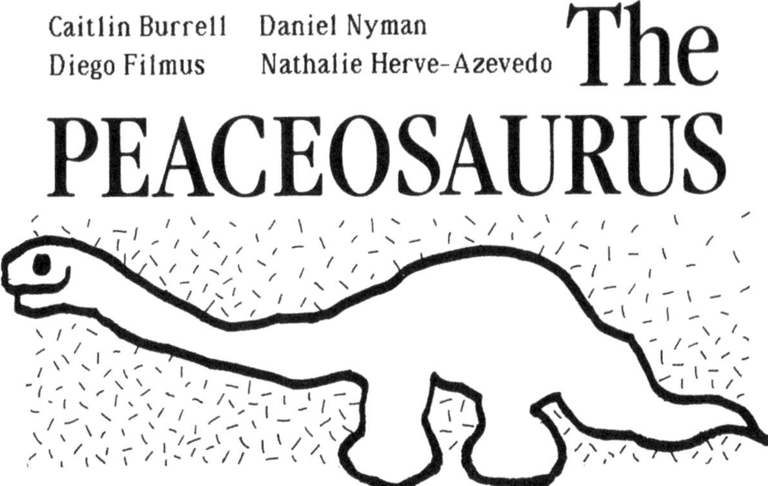

The DAS Peaceosaurus logo

We believe that DAS is the first public school in North America to have tried this in a formal way with such *young* children. We believe that we were pioneers, that our four oldest children who were in 3rd grade were the great explorers on this new expedition into the wilds of young children at recess, the first articulators, the documentarians. They wrote a book, *The Peaceosaurus* (Burrell, Nyman, Filmus, Herve-Azevedo, 1988). Another child (Katy Pandora Syperek) designed a logo. Both the book and the logo are named *The Peaceosaurus*. Then, a few years later, three DAS teachers wrote a book, *Children as Peacemakers* (Fine, Lacey, Baer, 1995). It was a fusion, a coming together, a realization. Everything was about peacemaking.

6

Another Flashback: The Hum

It's 1989. Judy Duncan, DAS educational assistant/art teacher, tells me that sometimes she hears a hum in the 3rd grade classroom. Quietly, which is her way, she waves me over to the art table, where a group of children are working with a student teacher who is helping them make miniature books (like chapbooks) from their stories, complete with illustrations and tiny print. The student teacher has shown them how to start with an 8 ½ by 11 inch piece of paper and fold fold fold until it is an actual book with pages that turn, no tape or stitching or staples required.

"Listen," whispers Judy. "Do you hear the hum? That's the sound of harmony. Every once in a while, when things are going perfectly in a classroom, you can hear that sound." Now I can hear it too. It's the sound of heaven on Earth, of harmony, of peace.

While such moments tend to be brief, I love that they hover as our ongoing possibility. I puzzle over the fact that human beings harmonize less frequently and less fully than they might. Of course that hum comes, goes, and mixes with all kinds of other sounds, but when we interview a group of the "ant funeral girls" years later in 2005 when they are in high school, they share a flurry of memories about teachers, about Judy and the art room, a game called "snack sneak," a gift they made for one of their lunchtime/afterschool care teachers when she left DAS, and on and on. All of them remember Ann with affection and tell us she was a great teacher. They especially loved the class trips to Ann's house near the open fields on Ward's Island where they could explore. What follows are a few examples of what they say as they re-live and imagine:

> **Alice:** There was a time I wanted to be a police officer and a clown and many things, singing, teaching … I think part of me, now I want to be a teacher, maybe a child and youth worker, work at a school like I go to now. One of my teachers really *gets me* now, and art therapy is something I could get into. I love to write, I'm putting together a poetry book, maybe writing on the side.
>
> **Tarah:** When I was young I always wanted to be teacher because of Ann and Lori. Over the past years it's changed a bit, I have a teacher this year who's really amazing, so he's influenced me to want to teach other people. I'm leaning towards that, or medicine. Like Hanna, I really like biology. I think all of us were really influenced by Judy the art teacher.
>
> **Another tells us:** I was making a paper crane the other day and thought of her [Judy]. I think of the art room, and there was paint everywhere. She worked at my mom's school for a while as an Ed. assistant and did the art program, and I remember when we did the winter solstice parade, every year we would make a castle. We would do it out of materials around school, egg cartons and toilet paper rolls. I still have the stuffed birds we made.

Sitting around a table in Molly's kitchen, as these high school girls reminisce about peacemaking, they talk about ways that each of them, in her own way, has taken this learning into her teenage life. Alice uses it with others in a group home setting; Molly says that although the formal rituals don't fit with a high-school social scene, the deeper understandings help her in day-to-day relationships. Qwyn talks about her work as a mediator, how she has been trained and called upon to help others as a volunteer at St. Stephens Community House ("The Arcade"). They may have dropped some of the formalities, but they haven't forgotten them or what they mean.

Lena's dove and peace signs

A typical schoolyard episode in the fall of 1994 focuses on a disagreement among a group of girls five to nine years of age. The conflict is about inclusion, exclusion, and who gets to decide the rules of the game.

During the peacemaking, kindergarten teacher Ann Lacey, along with the father of one of the girls [Hanna] supports these children as they try to sort out what has happened and come to understanding and agreement. They wipe their eyes, bicker and argue, try to define, never fully clarify for the adults, and eventually begin to giggle, crack jokes, and sing. Their eruption of joy is understood as a signal that resolution, whatever that might mean for these girls in this moment, has occurred. They end with a question, "How can we get Molly back into the game?" Then in chorus they chant, "I don't know, I don't know, I don't know." This serves as a moment of inclusion and they return to their game with all of them involved now.

Spontaneously, they begin dancing around a pole. The father [Rick] has been holding Molly on his lap throughout the peacemaking. She is not his daughter, though his own daughter [Hanna] has also been part of the conflict. He has held Molly, not because he is related to her, but because he understands that *she* is the one who needs to be embraced in order for the problem to resolve; he holds her because she is upset and needs extra care in this moment. The whole venture is collaborative.

A significant lesson can be found in the children's humor when a problem has been diffused or resolved. Sometimes the children begin to giggle and dance, and games resume with everyone included; adults learn to stand back, listen, watch, and protect only when necessary. They may not grasp quite how or why a resolution has occurred, but their knowing is not the main point. In filmed interviews, DAS teachers told us again and again that perfect resolution in adult terms is neither possible nor what really matters. What does matter is that the children are safe, that they express their feelings and opinions, hear each other's voices, and are supported as they exercise their own emergent sense of justice.

Often the film crew and I tried to follow six-year-old Maya both on and off the playground. Everywhere she ran (and she ran more than she walked), there was a flurry of activity. Maya seemed to move away from and toward conflict at the same time, not quite sure what she wanted. She was hard to keep up with, impossible to anticipate, and always worth the effort it took to keep trying. Where would her mind and her responses and her bouncing ponytail lead next? We couldn't predict, so on an early spring day in 1995, we hurried after her with camera and microphone and long cords.

"Help me! Help me," is the cry we hear as she and others race to Ann's side, perhaps more from a need to touch home base than from a need for protection. As their touchstone, Ann is gentle with Maya and Jessica who have brought yet another "problem" to her. They love bringing Ann problems. It's part of their relationship with each other and with Ann. They deliver problems, and Ann helps them articulate their "sides" and strategize solutions. "Take a deep breath and tell me what's happening," says Ann. "I want to know the content of the problem."

Jessica

"I don't know, it's kind of continuing from yesterday," explains Maya.

Ann tries to understand and sends her off to think, "Well, blow your nose and go for a walk and try to figure it out; if it doesn't work come back and see me," says Ann in a conversational voice. Maya wants to attract a group but is not sure how to make that happen. She wants to boost the action, she wants to be at the center of yet another collision, she wants to be wanted, all this at the same time. "Help me. Help me," rings out as Maya bolts away from Ann, propelled by the gift of teacherly advice, yet appearing to have forgotten Ann's message entirely.

Victoria Shearham describes the video footage of this confrontation as follows:

> Three girls begin to skip away from a wall. Maya grabs Jessica's arms and Jessica turns around, grabbing Maya's right arm. Maya calls out, "Hey!" Jessica pulls back her arm and pushes Maya away saying, "Don't! No."
>
> Maya, her arms at her sides, looks at Jessica. The third girl watches smiling. Jessica and Maya are standing a foot apart, watching each other. Jessica shakes her head and mutters something to Maya. Maya takes a step toward Jessica and grabs her shoulders. She squeezes Maya's shoulders and pushes her backwards slightly.
>
> "Why did you … trick me?!" Jessica asks. She walks forward, and Maya continues to walk backwards toward the wall. Jessica says, "You said you were playing and you're not." Jessica gives Maya a slight push and releases her grip, turning around to walk away.
>
> Maya skips after her saying, "Well you're …"
>
> Jessica turns around and Maya grabs her arms. The two girls

continue to mutter as Maya pushes Jessica. The third girl shouts, "Hey you guys," and attempts to separate the two, placing her hands on their chests and slightly pushing them apart. The girl then orders them to, "Cut it."

Jessica brushes off her hand as the girl repeats, "Cut it."

Maya cries, "Cut it yourself!" and pushes the girl away.

Maya turns to stomp off as the girl repeats, "Cut it yourself."

Maya is walking on the left of another girl, while Jessica is on the right. Quickly Jessica walks in front of the others to stop them. Maya walks away and Christine joins the group. Facing the other girl, Jessica lifts up her arms, throws them down again, and says, "I don't want … I just want to be alone, just me and Maya." The girls stare at each other for a second before Jessica walks off. The other girl looks at Christine.

Maya skips away after Jessica, her hands raised. "You don't have to be so nasty!" Maya screams, stopping in front of Jessica's face, her arms lowered. Jessica puts her hands on Maya's chest and pushes her away before running off again.

One of the other girls walks past Maya towards Jessica, "And you don't have to be so rude either!"

Christine walks up to Maya and says, "And you have to … and you don't have to yell … at her face." Maya is still standing looking at Jessica who is off in the distance.

Sticking out her tongue with an "mmm" sound, Maya walks over to a wrought iron and concrete fence behind which Jessica is playing by the jungle gym. Maya begins to scream, "Jessica! Since you're so nasty …"

Maya grabs the bars with her hands and rests her head between them, "I'm not your friend anymore!"

Three other girls, including Christine move in carefully behind Maya. Christine cautions, "Maya don't say that because someday you will want to be her friend again."

Maya runs after Jessica. Jessica takes a sharp right turn, and Maya follows, swinging her arms and screaming harsh words.

Another girl, who is running toward the two, quickly turns and runs calling out, "I'll go get Ann!" Jessica continues walking and Maya follows a few feet behind her and appears to be smiling as she clasps both hands to her mouth then swings them down again.

Ann sees them coming toward her. "Get over here," she growls in comedic style, coffee cup in hand. She leans toward them as the three girls approach. Jessica, frustrated, tosses her arms up and then throws them down again in an urgent sounding voice, trying to tell Ann that there is a problem, that "She [Maya] is trying to make a problem."

The girl who went to fetch Ann is standing off to her left. A few others still hover. Maya (her hands in her pockets) and Jessica are now standing in front of Ann who asks, "What happened?" Maya looks behind her, and Jessica turns her body slightly to look away from Ann. "Because I'm clueless," Ann continues.

Jessica throws up her hands in frustration and yells, "I just told you! She's trying to make a problem!"

"About what?" Ann asks.

"She's just …" Jessica begins.

Ann says, "I want to know the content of the problem."

Jessica, now close to tears is yelling, "She's just … saying stuff, like things that would be in a problem and she's trying to make a problem, that's all!"

"Ok, can you stop screaming?" asks Ann. "It makes it really hard to listen to you."

Jessica takes a quick breath and starts jumping up and down, waving her arms, "I can't sto-op!" She bites her bottom lip, still upset.

"Well then go away from me and blow your nose," Ann says, passing Jessica a tissue. "And I'll talk to Maya."

"Ok," Jessica says taking the tissue and holding it to her nose before walking away.

Ann, facing Maya, asks, "What's happening?"

Maya, looks at the ground, raises her arms, and shrugs, "Well, I don't know." She looks around, her face scrunched up.

There is a long pause. Ann asks, "What happened, that Jessica's talking about?" Maya looks toward where Jessica was and rolls her head the other direction saying, "Well …"

Ann interjects, "You were there."

Maya raises her arms and continues, "We were in a fight yesterday remember?"

"Ya," Ann replies.

Maya continues, arms at her sides, "And, and it's sort of continuing today too." She looks down at her feet.

Ann bends down toward Maya, "Do you have any idea why it's continuing?"

Maya shrugs, "I don't know."

Ann asks, "Did you really think about it? Think about if someone was doing it to you."

Maya puts her hands in her pockets and looks away from Ann, "I would be mad."

She looks back at Ann who asks, "What would you want them to say to you?"

Maya begins, "I would say, like …"

> "Just walk about the playground and think about that," Ann suggests.
>
> Maya goes on, "I would say . . . I want to play with my friends too. What if you can play with your friends and I can play with you with your friends too?"
>
> Ann answers, "Think of a kind way to say it and see if it works, try it out."
>
> "Ok," Maya replies, turning from Ann and starting to walk away in Jessica's direction.
>
> "Come back if it's a problem still," Ann offers.
>
> Maya skips off, swinging her arms, as she moves toward Jessica, who is now standing far off in a corner. They eye each other, and for no clear reason someone yells, "Help me! Help me!" Maya stops and holds out her arms, appearing confused as she watches Jessica run off.
>
> Ann, watching from afar, looks at the camera and says, "They're frisky today."

Viewing the video and reading the description that Victoria made, I wonder if, rather than a problem, this might perhaps be a drama, an unclear game these girls don't quite know how to play safely without support from their kindergarten teacher. Quite possibly, Ann has been cast in a role that she isn't fully aware of, but is nevertheless able to perform with grace, wit, and wisdom.

In an earlier episode (spring 1995), this time inside their kindergarten classroom, Maya, while somewhat quieter then, is at the center of a conflict. It is building time. Hanna, Qwyn, Molly, Maya and others have been working at a table together creating "structures." When Ann announces that it is time to clean up, Maya becomes overly zealous and knocks over Hanna's structure. Hanna is furious with Maya, and a heated argument ensues. She and other girls begin to prod and probe Maya about where her mother works. The Bank of Montreal? Impossible in their minds. She can't work "at" Montreal, Molly tells her (because of course they see her in Toronto, at school, every day at 3:30).

Maya manages to hold her own and finally, with a shrug, she gives up on what we now know (from conversations with these girls many years later) was a misunderstanding.

"Does your mother really work in the Bank 'at' Montreal?" asks Molly.

"Yes," replies Maya.

"No," insist the others.

"She's a liar," says Hanna.

In 2011 we bring participants and guests together for a conference at the Lillian Smith Branch, Toronto Public Library. Maya and her mother attend, sit on a panel, and field questions. Someone asks them about the Bank of Montreal dispute, and they explain. Finally, the truth; Maya was not lying. Why would she lie about such a thing? Hanna knew that Maya's mother couldn't possibly have worked "at Montreal" because Montreal is five hours away by car.

We now know first-hand from the adult Maya and her mother, who was still employed there in 2011, that she did work *at* the "Bank *of* Montreal," and that part of the confusion was in the wording. Words words words. So ambiguous, so provocative; words are the power tool in this fairly quiet bullying episode. Words are also the power tool in peacemaking.

Molly has used the word "at" in her four-year-old voice "Does your mother really work in the Bank *at* Montreal?"

Hanna corrects her, "Bank *of* Montreal."

Hanna's frustration at Maya's having demolished her structure before she had time to show it to Ann, and her accusation, "You're a liar," contributed to the escalation of an indoor fight. This led to a throwing down of blocks and harsh words that they all remember vividly years later.

While we saw ongoing conflicts and confrontations, we also witnessed many examples of collaboration among children at work and play.

Dale & Nick

Victoria Shearham describes a cooperative scene between two little boys who are serious about baseball (spring 1994):

> Dale, clutching a baseball in his right hand and a catcher's mitt in his left, issues orders like an old coach. He points to his friend Nick, "OK, you're catcher." As a gesture of acceptance, Dale's companion turns his cap around. In order to inform his friend of the proper way to play baseball, Dale begins to question him, "Know signals? Know the signals?"

Ignoring the question—purposely or otherwise—the other boy proceeds to take the glove from Dale.

Unshaken by Nick's apparent lack of enthusiasm for the semi-traditional gestures of baseball, Dale leans in and demonstrates the signals. Unfortunately, Nick finds something on his shoe that is of more interest and bends down to tug at his sock.

Not yet moved by this recent setback, Dale stretches out his right arm and pokes his friend with his left, "You know, you know when they do this?" Another tap. Nick looks up. "You know when catchers do this?"

Nick examines his shoe. Dale leans over to make sure his gesture can be clearly seen, "You know, that's a pitch out." In a last ditch attempt to awaken some gusto in his friend, Dale pretends to throw a pitch. His friend is still focusing on his shoes.

Finally Nick stands up. Without another word, the boys begin to back away from one another. Uncertain of his friend's readiness as catcher, Dale directs, "Kneel down like a catcher. Go like that!" The boy complies. Still not quite right, Dale calls out, "Nick, come forward! Come on, give me the signal." Dale, hands on his knees, rocks back on his heels in anticipation of Nick's call.

Nick cries, "Go!" But it's still not quite right.

Dale crouches down and holds his hand on the ground. "Go like this," he shouts before standing up. "Give me the signal," Dale insists. Nick, still crouching on the ground, remains silent. "Give me the signal," Dale repeats.

Nick finally responds, "What is it?"

With steady patience Dale repeats his hand gestures adding a few minor changes and asks Nick, "What do you want now? Do you want a fast-ball?"

> Nick, in a half-hearted attempt to follow the hand signals, gives up and replies, "Curve-ball."
>
> Dale walks to his imaginary pitcher's mound and issues a final warning call, "And get ready, 'cause my curve goes …"
>
> Dale prepares for the wind up. With determination he attempts to mimic a pro baseball pitcher—his leg is raised, his right hand clutches the ball and stretches backwards, his left arm thrusts ahead, his hand tenses. Dale is building up momentum now. He takes one step forward, two steps forward and he … stops. "Kneel down!" he calls. Nick quickly drops to the ground, catcher's mitt at the ready in front of him.
>
> "Throw it!" Nick cries. In agreement, Dale nods his head and, reassuming his pitcher's pose, he sends the ball flying! Unfortunately, it appears that this throw is a real curve ball as the ball travels in a gentle arc toward Nick.
>
> Unhappy with the result, Dale proclaims, "That was a bad knuckle-ball!" Nick, having found the ball, uses his whole body to send it flying back to Dale. Reaching up as high as he can Dale just misses the ball. Now to retrieve it and try one more throw.

In the video that Victoria describes, the children throw, they miss, they drop and chase and retrieve. Despite all their sincere efforts, they never manage to catch a single ball.

Of course not all play is so cooperative and trouble-free. In another interaction (early March 1994), this one inside the 2nd – 3rd grade classroom, Christine is in tears. Teacher Lori McCubbin attempts to console her as she tries to find out what has gone wrong. Lori encourages Christine to dry her eyes and face the friends who have hurt her feelings. Lori agrees to sit with Christine and the group for a peacemaking.

Victoria Shearham describes the video footage of this interaction as follows:

> Savannah is holding court with a small group of children who are sitting on the floor in front of her.
>
> "Can I say something?" one girl asks.
>
> Savannah, with great exaggeration, replies, "Jane no, it's not your show and tell." She rolls her eyes, which prompts some chuckles from the group. The children look up at Savannah as she announces, "I'm going to pick; who wants to be second? Put up your hand if you want to be second."
>
> Dutifully, the children raise their hands, but a lone voice speaks up, "No, you have to follow the board."
>
> Savannah, ignoring the upstart comment, looks at one of the children in the group and proclaims, "K. gets the second act."
>
> Christine, who is sitting amongst some chairs on top of a table, yells out, "How come I was talking and you talked?" Christine's voice begins to quiver, and she becomes very upset as she continues, "Well it doesn't mean you have to interrupt. I didn't interrupt yours!"
>
> Savannah (with crossed arms) and Jane are now sitting on a table nearby. Jane looks over her shoulder and adds, "And anyways Christine, we're sorry."
>
> Jane's words appear to have no effect on the still visibly upset Christine who raises her shoulders and lowers her head to look at the ground.
>
> Lori looks over from across the room and begins walking toward the girls. She crouches down next to an upset Christine who is wiping her eyes with her sleeve. "If you can't get Savannah to listen to you ..." Lori begins.
>
> Christine interrupts, "Jane wasn't ..." Voice trailing off, she

rubs her eye.

“And Jane,” Lori says, reaching up to push back some hair that has wandered onto Christine’s face. Christine plays with the leg of the chair in front of her. “If they’re not listening to you,” Lori prods, “what can you do?”

Christine looks at Lori. “Go and talk to the teacher?” she asks.

Lori replies, “Get an adult to help you, because sometimes when people don’t listen it’s totally frustrating. And if they’re not listening, you need some help. So take a breath, take a breath.” Christine takes a couple of deep breaths. “Do you think you’re ready to … tell them what you need?” Lori asks.

Christine shakes her head from side to side. “Because Jane took over,” Christine says, laying her head down on her arm. “She’s doing her show and tell.”

Jane, unaware of the upset her show and tell has caused, is in the midst of presenting the cards she is holding to the class. Smiling, Jane holds one of the cards up, “And I got this from Ethan.” Looking at both cards Jane continues, “And, they’re very special.”

Lori, still crouched in front of the tearful Christine, says, “That doesn’t mean we can’t stop it. You ready? Or do you want to calm down?”

Christine wipes her face with her arm and mutters into her sleeve, “I want you to … help me.”

Lori, understanding this quiet request, says, [to the group] “Excuse me, I’m going to interrupt you.” Lori sits down on a stool near Jane. Christine and Jane are now standing with Lori, and soon two other girls join, one of whom is Savannah. “Sit down,” Lori insists, taking Christine’s hand and gently guiding her toward the floor. Savannah moves to the chair, but Jane and the other girl remain standing. “Sit down please,” Lori repeats firmly, looking at Jane. The other girl sits on the floor, but Jane crouches down.

Lori holds Christine's hand in her lap, as if to comfort her and asks, "Do you want to tell?" Lori looks at Jane and the other girls, "Christine needs to talk to you."

"I don't …" Christine begins in a whisper, but apparently not everyone is prepared to listen attentively.

Lori chimes in, looking at Savannah, "I don't see you looking at Christine."

All the girls look up at Savannah, but they quickly turn back to Christine who tells her side of the story in a low, trembling voice, "I didn't like it when you interrupted me when I was trying to say something." Christine's upset bubbles to the surface as her voice cracks and she begins to cry.

"Sorry Christine," Jane says.

Lori, who has been watching the other girls, looks back at Christine and says, "Can you tell them about the part … do you remember what you said to me first?" Christine takes a breath, but remains quiet while Lori continues, "About how you were behaving during show and tell?"

Through her tears Christine manages to say, "I was listening to Savannah's, and then—she didn't listen—she [wasn't] listening to mine, she was talking."

Lori replies with a "Hmm," and Christine takes a short breath before wiping her face with her sleeve.

Jane takes this moment to tell her side of the story, "Well … I wasn't interrupting Savannah, but I was telling the kids what I did *with* Savannah."

Lori tries to interpret for them, "But I think what Christine's trying to explain to you is that she tried to listen to what you had to say, and then when it was her turn," she looks at Christine, "no one listened to her. She was feeling really frustrated because she couldn't get people to listen. You know how that feels?"

Jane looks at Lori, "You didn't really mean to."

Lori nods, "That's true." She looks at Christine who is still sitting next to her. "Do you hear that?" Lori asks, "How does that make you feel when she says she's sorry?" Jane, seemingly unfazed by the drama, plays with the cards in her hands.

There is a pause, which is interrupted by Christine who mutters, "A little better."

"A little better?" Lori repeats, glancing at the girls briefly before looking back at Christine, "What, what can these two do to make it feel really better?"

She gives the trio in front of her a slight nod as Christine whispers, "Listen."

Jane, apparently satisfied with this proposal, jumps up and says, "Okay."

Lori asks intently, "Think you can do it?"

If we consider Victoria's description of the video footage in light of the later interviews with Christine and Savannah, one in 1996 (phase 1 year 3) and the next in 2004 (phase 2), we learn a lot about what they think, see, hear, remember and ponder later on. The following are excerpts from the phase 1 and phase 2 interviews.

We interviewed Savannah and Christine separately when they were in fourth grade (1996):

Savannah: You know how in peacemaking, when everyone feels comfortable, we go on to solutions. And, that's, but that's, only when everyone feels that the problem is solved. And the problem is solved when ... say someone gets called a name, or something, they get up to that point when they feel ... like I called someone a name, or something, and they were mad at me and I said ... well, I'm sorry. Like sorry, or something like that. That's not really saying sorry. Because you're saying it in a rude way. And it like, if you're saying it in a rude way, that shows that you're still, like angry at the person. So maybe when they say it in a nice voice, and the person actually believes that they mean it, maybe that's probably, when they want to go onto solutions and start talking about what they could do next time to prevent the problem.

Christine: Usually when everybody, says like, what happened, we usually go onto solutions, and then when we're done we usually ask, like, if we are friends again or something. And if they say, the problem isn't solved yet, I don't think it is. Then um, they, we, like, talk some more. Or if … they think it's solved, then they just shake hands and make up … it's usually solved but not always. Like some people, it takes a long time with some people cuz they have, like, a lot of things to say to them, or they don't think it's solved. Sometimes, it's just like, when someone talks behind someone's back cuz a lot of people don't like that and then they get really mad at them and they start, like some people just start yelling at them, and stuff like that, and then it gets into a big problem and … like sometimes, I think it was last year, I got into a big fight with my friend and we didn't talk to each other for [long pause] one-and-a-half days.

Savannah: You can't go through 4th grade, or any grade without having at least two fights or something like that. But I don't think I'll ever get into a real physical fight cuz I'm not really that kind of person. Like, I don't, I don't usually yell a lot either at my friends when I'm in a fight … [I] just like, talk really firmly to them and make them understand. I don't like, yell a lot. I cry sometimes, but I don't, like, yell a lot. I don't like make it physical or anything like that.

We interviewed Savannah and Christine again in high school (2004):

Years later, when Savannah and Christine were in high school, we interviewed them again, and this time they were together, in Christine's family home. They had not gone to the same school since DAS, but they had maintained contact. Here they reminisce about their relationship as children, and they talk about how they still use peacemaking principles in their high school environments:

> **Christine:** Savannah was a very leadership-type person. [*Savannah chuckles softly*] And I guess, I kinda was the same, so it was easy for us to, you know, to be together because we were so much alike. [*Savannah nods*] Sometimes we butted heads cuz we wanted, you know, to be like, the lead in our play or whatever.
>
> **Savannah:** Yeah.
>
> **Christine:** But we're both very much like that. So it was easy to be, like, together because we would always come up with ideas that were similar 'n' stuff cuz we both wanted to do the same thing, so it was very easy for us to be friends.
>
> **Christine:** We used to do plays.
>
> **Savannah:** We always did plays.
>
> **Christine:** We always did plays and made scripts and stuff like that.
>
> **Savannah:** And I choreographed ballets for everyone.
>
> **Christine:** And we did the music and everything. At lunch we would all come together and we'd, like do a scene or something like that. It wasn't actually shown to anybody but … [*Turns to Savannah*] do you remember us being cheerleaders that one time?
>
> **Savannah:** Yes, yes.
>
> **Christine:** And we ummm had pompoms made out of um …
>
> **Savannah:** Garbage bags [*Both laugh*]

Christine: We shredded them and taped them together. We had uniforms and stuff like that.

Savannah: Yah, I remember that.

Christine: That was pretty funny.

Christine: I loved DAS. It was, I felt, I guess, more [safe], than I do at [regular] school because I knew everybody and they would like, protect me from anything. So it's a lot different in [other schools]. [*Savannah nods*] Like I went to a middle school, a [regular school] in 5,6,7,8 and it was a lot different. It was like, when I learned I had to call them [the teachers] by their last names, I was like, "Okay, that's a little weird." [*Savannah nods*] Like in DAS, it was more of a community, you knew everyone by their first names.

Savannah: Um hm.

Christine: And it was really, it felt very impersonal to talk to my teacher because I had to call them "Sir" and "Mrs." [*Savannah nods*] And it was like very closed-off I guess, they were kinda closed-off. They weren't approachable as much as they were in DAS. [*Savannah nods*]

Savannah: I think I learned a lot about problem solving from the school and even just like, the atmosphere was really good. With like, I mean you have the odd student that you don't like or the odd teacher you don't like. That's always going to happen, but overall it was a really great experience for me.

Christine: I do remember them showing us how … they would make us do little skits. Like they would show us, they would model it for us, [*Savannah nods*] and then they would … give us a situation or something like that, and then we would almost have to [do a] role play of what we would do.

The girls recall being taught and periodically reminded of the process, the steps.

Christine: Yah. They would, they would always … every year they kinda reminded us of how to do it just so that it was always fresh in our minds.

Savannah: I even remember, like they let us take time out of class if we had a really big problem. Then, like, some of us could go out in the hall and we'd actually have our peacemaking circle … it's not like they taught it to us and didn't let us use it. They, they, encouraged us to take time if we needed to, to solve our problems.

The girls tell each other about how they now try to share what they know about peacemaking with high school classmates, encouraging friends to "talk it over" instead of using "the silent treatment." They explain mediation, why you sometimes need a mediator, so that, as Christine explains, things don't get "out of hand," and so that problems can be solved more quickly.

Savannah tells us about her arts-focus high school, a public school that, while not designated as an alternative school, doesn't feel like a "regular" public school. She says that even with her friends there, some of them don't solve their problems and just kind of pretend that "nothing happened":

Savannah: [*Turns to Christine*] I don't know if you find that?

Christine: Yah. It happens all the time.

Savannah: I don't like doing that at all. Like I don't, I can't just …

Christine: It kinda eats away at you.

Savannah: Yah. And I, I kind of, I like to talk about my problems and try to figure them out so that there's no awkwardness between me and my friends, but a lot of them just pretend like nothing happened, and that really bothers me sometimes.

Christine tells us that her experiences with peacemaking have probably made her friendly, more open to other people and their opinions, and a less angry person than she might otherwise have been. She says, "I know how to deal with my problems because I was taught at a very young age how to do it."

Eight years later in 2004, both Savannah and Christine still remember one "huge" fight they had with each other when they were young children at DAS.

Here are some things they told us about that fight when we interviewed them (separately) years earlier in 1996 when they were in 4th grade:

> **Savannah as a child:** We had clip boards that we had to check off things that we had to do, like every week and things. And ummm well, what we used to do when we got in fights cuz we couldn't really talk to each other because we were in different classes. So what we did was, umm, we would write notes to each other.
>
> **Christine as a child:** And what she did was she wrote a note about it. Like um, like she wanted to say sorry and all that. So she put a note on my clipboard and I usually get notes there. So I picked it up and she said, I'd like to, I wanna work this out and I'm really sorry. And so we, umm go to a private place and we work it out.
>
> **Savannah as a child:** And I said something like, "I've known you for a long time and I don't wanna, like, stop being friends right now, and I really like you so can we try to get back together?" So, it's been getting easier and easier because we've learned over the years how each, each one of us, like, knows how to peacemake and how it's the easiest way to peacemake with us. Most of them were misunderstandings, but then some of them are just fights; we get mad at each other for doing something or something like that.

They remember this again as teenagers during the interview together in 2004

Savannah: So we were having a problem and Lori talked to me about it. I remember. And then, I wrote you a poem. Do you remember?

Christine: Right, I think I have that somewhere.

Savannah: I had a poem and then … a letter. I remember that.

Christine: Yah.

Savannah: Lori, actually, was the one who, I think … actually encouraged me to do it. She knew. That's the thing, she saw right away. Cuz, we were, like, best friends.

Christine: Yah, we were really close.

Savannah: And she saw that we were having problems, and I think I was really upset about it, and so [Lori] came to talk to me about it and she said, "Why don't you try this?" And I wrote you that poem about something, bicycles and stuff like that. [*Both laugh*] I dunno.

Christine tells us about conflicts at her next schools. She says:

Christine: We were like so used to just solving our problems, and *they* [others at her high school] "solve" their problems by screaming at each other. It was kind of scary almost. But, I mean, I still tried to keep the peacemaking thing with me throughout the whole thing. They had different approaches to dealing with problems, and they wanted to do it their way so it was kind of hard to solve a problem other than what I knew. So, that was always a little different, solving my problem a different way than what I was used to, cuz they were used to other things. I'm in grade 11, and high school, it's … so much different. It's a lot more violent. Like, people don't really know how to resolve issues or anything like that. I mean, I get really scared going to school sometimes because just recently we had a stabbing at my school. And so, I mean, I don't understand why people wouldn't just solve their problems. You know?

Flashback - A pretend peacemaking turns "real" (December 1994):

(Christine, Savannah, Midori, Jasmine, and Others)

A small group of 2nd – 3rd grade girls are playing a game. It is a "pretend peacemaking" in rehearsal mode for a skit they have been preparing. Not all of the girls who were planning to be in the skit are in the room during this game. When Midori enters she is upset, thinking she has been left out of an actual rehearsal, rather than a "pretend rehearsal."

MIDORI ENTERS, ELLI PEEKS IN. MIDORI BEGINS TO CRY, AND A **REAL** PEACEMAKING ENSUES. SPONTANEOUSLY THE GIRLS FORM A CIRCLE. CHRISTINE SITS NEXT TO MIDORI AND TAKES THE LEAD.

Child 1: Are you in it?

Child 2: Yup, I'm a peacemaker.

Christine: Do you agree to solve it, with us or a peacemaker?

[*Several students say "Peacemaker" and "Peacemakers"*]

Christine: Who wants to go first? [*Savannah and Jasmine raise their hands.*]

Savannah: Um well. We, were um like. We were doing this play and Midori was in it we did it for the camera people and then at the end when Midori came in. I forget who it was but someone told her that ummm we did the play without her. So Midori got really frustrated about it.

Jasmine: Midori, I told you, that I reacted silly in the play. So it wouldn't be the real play. But, I told you. And I told you it wasn't the real play. And then you got all upset and then you started laughing. And then, and then you came back and, and now it's another problem.

Christine: Do you want to say anything?

Jasmine: We already solved it.

Christine: Not if she feels sad.

Jasmine: She wasn't sad in there when we were still doing it. [*Points*] She was laughing. And she had a smile. She wasn't frowning like this.

Christine: [*Taps Midori*] Wanna say anything?

Midori: [*Timidly, almost crying*] Well, it's not fair that you got to do it in front of the camera and I didn't.

Jasmine: Well, we acted silly to tell you the truth. [*Looks to Savannah*] We didn't really, we didn't really. Yah we laughed and went: [*Mimics herself acting silly earlier, by putting fingers and wiggles them in front of her face*] Agrahaha! Agrahaha! And it wasn't really the serious [Play].

Christine: Midori, why did you feel sad? [*Pats Midori on the hair*] Did you … cuz, I'm a little mixed up. Cuz when we came to do the peacemaking Jasmine was sort of yelling. That's why you felt sad?

Midori: No.

Jasmine: I didn't yell, I said, Midori, I, I, I … I told her that we have already satisfied it. I told her, like, like, five times that we did not do the real play. It was just really funny.

Another child puts her hand up and says: Yah she was kinda being silly so I went like that [*Nods head*] and she was like, aahhh I'm scared. [*Pretends to grab on to someone*] So that wasn't really what she was supposed to do.

Jasmine: See it wasn't a real play. It was really "raaaaaaa."

[*Waves index finger in circles and smiles*]

Christine: So what you are doing is laughing so I think you made up! [*Smiles*]

The children double cross their arms and all join hands in the middle of the circle to signify that the pretend-peacemaking-turned-real has come to a close and resolution has been reached.

7

More Than Twelve Years Later: Excerpts From Interviews With Kids

We interviewed Dale (2005):

Years later in June of 2005 when we interviewed Dale (baseball Dale from Chapter 6) in his family home, he was in his final days of high school. He tells us what he remembers about the operations of peacemaking at DAS, and he speaks openly of his complex life since elementary school:

Dale: "Peacemaking was a big part of DAS."

> I remember from early on that peacemaking was a big part of DAS and it was like the kids solving their own problems. You get two people and then you get peacemakers, either one or two people that help you out … sometimes it was like a really big problem; you might go to people older than you, I think, and then if it was really, really big then the teacher would obviously come in. Other than that I think it was just like the peacemakers would try and make sure that both sides got heard … first one person would tell their side, then the other person would tell their side, then the peacemakers would … come up with solutions that they can both agree to … so it was like a non-violent conflict resolution.
>
> Dale tells us he "liked it a lot." He recalls that "it worked pretty well." He says:
>
> The ideal of it was really really important and something that's still ingrained in me now as something that has stayed with me … overall just the idea of not using violence to "solve" problems, which was what it was all about, and just using words and stuff. That's what I remember most about it and just the principles behind peacemaking and not necessarily the process itself.

Dale calls it a "teaching method, like letting kids have a voice and having people being able to speak out … a very empowering sort of education."

Dale remembers a DAS teacher, Mark, from when he was a bit older. He says, "One time Mark brought … this new sort of peacemaking style … sometimes the class would have a problem … he'd talk to us as a class. We always had little circles … if there was a bigger problem, or just something that he wanted to discuss with the class, then we'd share it there."

Dale had a less positive experience in his next school immediately following 6th grade. He says that when he left DAS he experienced "culture shock." He goes on to tell us about some of his struggles:

> I don't think the school was the reason, but actually I had a really, really bad time in grade 7 and 8. It was just something that I went through … it was a really tough time for me. At that time I was having a lot of anxiety attacks.

For high school Dale chose the same large downtown school that his older brother was attending. He explains that:

> [My] brother was still at Bloor Collegiate, being only three years older than me. So, that was really helpful, having someone older in the school that I knew, and so I knew other people because of that and, I don't know … Bloor seemed the place to go.

Another factor for Dale was that he wanted a school with sports teams (remember he loved baseball even when he was in Lori's 2nd – 3rd grade class). He tells us:

> At Bloor I played on both the baseball and hockey teams and I was able to play on the hockey team with my brother
>
> After I'm done high school, I'm planning to go to either U. of T. [University of Toronto] or University of Waterloo … into math and I wanna become a math teacher—high school math teacher. Early on I had thought I wanted to be a teacher … early, like when I was in elementary school.
>
> My dad is a high school chemistry teacher … and his mom was a teacher as well, and so was my great aunt, so teaching is in the family … I hope to be a teacher who can be very versatile and just teach, like, you know, basically teach my lesson and then … if a student needs help, be able to come at it from an approach that will work for them.

We interviewed Elli (1994):

We interviewed Elli twice—first in 1994 when she was in 1st grade, and again in June 2005 when she was about to graduate from high school. Both times her mother Sharon was at her side. The 1994 interview (Fine, 1997) took place after school at DAS. Elli and her mother try to recall how Elli first learned about peacemaking:

Question: When did you first hear about peacemaking, do you remember?

Elli: When I first came to this school.

Question: And how was it described to you? How did it present itself?

Elli: They described it as helping you solve … your problems, and helping [you] get along a little more with your problems.

Question: And how was it done in the school? How was it used?

Elli: Well, if there was a problem, any kind of problem, which even if it was a really small problem and the kids could just say it to each other, and figure it out, they didn't need a big peacemaking, and if it was a problem that sort of was … following into the class, you would try to solve it, and if that didn't work then you would solve it with the teacher.

Question: And were there a lot of problems that were solved?

Elli: Not too many when I first came.

Question: [What] was your first experience? Did you have a problem that got solved or … did you work as a …

Elli: Um, my first experience was being a peacemaker.

Question: And how did that go?

Elli: Fine.

Question: What was involved with that?

Elli: I don't remember, it was a pretty long time ago.

Question: Have you learned more and more about peacemaking … as you've gone through?

Elli: Yeah, because as you get older they … let you do more and more problems. Like, when you're in kindergarten they don't have you like blast out a lot of problems and like be peacemaker for like a lot and lot and lot of problems; [they] usually have the older kids do that.

Question: So, what kind of things did you learn as you got more familiar with it and you started to do it more …?

Elli: Well, there were some [things] that excited me … one day, when … my class and [the other] class were going to watch a movie … I was called by Ann [Ann Lacey, kindergarten teacher], and she said, there's a problem with, like older kids, really older kids, from [the other] room, and she said, could you come … and solve it, and I was, uh, one of the first kids to actually go into an older class and figure out that problem.

So, it felt good … first you ask, "Do you wanna solve the problem?" And then, "Do you wanna solve it with us or the teacher?" 'Cause sometimes the kids say, "Well I need the teacher 'cause this is a problem I can't do with kids."

Sometimes they say "This is ok to do with kids…" [And] then they say their sides. You ask one kid their side and the other kid says their side. And then you ask, "Are you ready for solutions?" If the kid says yes and the other kid says, no, I still need to talk about my feelings, then you [talk about] the feelings until it's okay with everybody to do solutions.

Then you do solutions. Then [if somebody] says, "Yes that solution's ok with me," you ask if their problem's solved. If they both say "Yes," you cross hands and you shake them and the problem's finished.

> Well … it happened outside, there's a lot of problems that happen outside, so we came in and this isn't something usual, but sometimes your teacher sits you down in a big circle around on the carpet and then the people who are in [the] problem and the peacemakers sit in the middle, and the teacher and all the kids … listen to the problem and then everybody in the whole circle can think of solutions.
>
> And then you can ask kids in the circle, too, but … if one person in the problem says, "No, that would be a little too, like, scary for me," or, "It would shock me a little," you would go out, and then you go somewhere else, and you don't do it with so many kids.

As a young child Elli saw the peacemaking process as flexible and adaptable to what people seemed to need at the time. She appeared proud of what she knew and pleased with how she could contribute to the process. She didn't recall too much about conflicts she herself may have had with others; at this early stage, she seemed to understand more about her role as a developing peacemaker who wanted to help others and play an important role in the school community.

When children read, write and talk about what matters to them most, their interactions lead them to shared discoveries in areas crucial to their lives. When teachers and parents do these things, their learning can parallel that of the children. Therefore, parents were also encouraged to learn about, and become involved in, peacemaking. Elli's mother participated in workshops designed by DAS teachers to familiarize parents with peacemaking and to encourage them to practice and make use of it within the family at home (Fine, 1997).

We interviewed Elli again (2005):

Our second interview with Elli and her mother took place many years later in 2005, in the senior English classroom at the alternative school from which she was about to graduate. We also interviewed her English teacher Rob Shoub, who was at the time a graduate student of mine at York University. The world seemed round, full-circle round, to me on that afternoon, and I am astonished at some of the similarities between the later interview and the one when Elli was in Lori's 2nd – 3rd grade class. Here are selected segments from the transcript of our conversation with Elli in high school and her mother Sharon. They talk of important learnings they took with them from DAS:

> **Elli:** The skills of I-messages and not using you-messages, the skills of taking care of feelings, and the skill of compromising … that I learned at DAS and throughout all my other schools, is something that you take to all the different aspects of your life. And you use that to understand yourself … potentially good and bad situations … you use it to navigate.

> **Elli:** Often when a problem was solved it started mending itself. It's not like the next day we were all perfect and all friends, but again our feelings were taken care of and so we worked our way away from them. So, if it re-occurred a couple times, that would be because it wasn't a time of adjustment; we all had bad habits—that were some things that you have when you get a problem. And, I think that's translated into my life. I know that if I have a problem with someone and we talk about it, [the problems] don't need to change the next day, it's ok for that change to take some time. The important thing is that [we're] trying. And I think that's something I got from the peacemaking at DAS. If it didn't work the first time, you "peacemaked" it again, and that was perfectly ok 'cause that's human interaction, but we kept

working at it until [it] got better, and that's so wonderful.

Sharon: I didn't want boundaries between home and school, and that was another reason why DAS was so appealing. The approach I guess I was looking for because of the theatre work I had done with young people and the realization that all learning is … risk taking and you need to be in a safe environment where your opinion is valued and where you learn to value everyone's opinion … I remember sitting out in the playground with Ann Lacey and just watching the kids … and what was going on there … the playground tells you a lot about how things are, how the kids treat each other. And one child came up to Ann and was crying and she was telling her about the problem she was having with her best friends—her two best friends. Ann listened and then she suggested, "Well, is there … could you go to another friend that might take care of you right now?" And the kid thought a second and said, "Oh ya, I could," and off she went, and this is a, you know, kindergarten child. And … the concept of starting to take responsibility for your feelings and your own problems, it seemed … such a sophisticated idea.

Elli: You didn't interrupt one another, you listened to each other's ideas, you made sure that everyone felt listened to. The first thing you did before you did a peacemaking was you made sure both sides agreed there was a problem, and this is so important 'cause if one person doesn't know [or acknowledge] there's a problem, how can you go about solving it? So you made sure both people agreed there was a problem and that they wanted to solve it. You never went into a peacemaking not wanting to.

Elli: And just to relate that to what I do in my life now, if I have a problem I know it's important to wait to solve it until I'm in a [the right] space. You don't try and push the solving right then for a quick fix solution, and that's definitely something that I learned from that. You wait 'till people are ready to solve it. Then, before you bring them together, you talk to them individually and you see, you know, make them feel heard … not forcing the solution … the process being the important part, not necessarily that you find a solution … both people acknowledge there's a problem, both people are ready to solve the problem, making sure both sides feel listened to, both from the peacemakers and from each other. If that can't happen you wait [during the peacemaking]. You make sure everyone feels listened to before you move on to the problem solving stage.

Elli: When you get to the problem solving stage, you do brainstorming; you think of different solutions … then you go on to finding the compromise, but you check … if you're not [everyone's not] ready to go on to the compromise you might have to go back to the beginning and start all over again, but you keep going with the people who are in the problem … you make sure that you don't favor one person or the other over who's being more emotional. You know that if both people are in a problem, they both need to be taken care of and a peacemaker needs to stay neutral—something taught to us at a very young age, which is a great skill to learn. And then finally you get to the compromise, you make sure everyone feels heard and basically, when you go through all that, sometimes you didn't even get to the compromise or the solution, but it was enough to be heard and that was the solution.

Sharon: I spoke with Lori and we thought that it would be an interesting experience to give the kids some creative dance movement … I normally work with much older kids so I was … making new workshops and then the kids of course would help me so I wasn't really worried … I gathered together a bunch of materials that I [thought] would intrigue the kids and I made a tape of lots of different kinds of music … the kids were amazing.

8
Teacher Voices

We interviewed teachers Marie, Lori, and Ann on a regular basis during the 1993-1996 phase when the children were in elementary grades. Ten years later we met with them again to learn how their teaching had evolved, and about influences the DAS experience might be having on their more recent work.

From the phase 1 interviews with Marie (1993-1996):

In after school interviews Marie talked about her 4th – 6th grade program at DAS. She also articulated her understandings of peace-making. She wisely reminds us that conflict is an ongoing fact of life, and that there will always be disagreements. Marie says:

> They're going to argue … and children deal with it a little differently than adults, they don't rationalize as [easily], or they don't … use their logic … they don't know how to manage anger as quickly, I think, as we might … so, they lash out a lot faster … you have to be realistic too, about what to expect from them … I think I'm getting more that way too as I … teach longer … you begin to accept some of this, but not in a way that you're going to let it happen … you're going to deal with it differently in a more realistic way. You know, you become less idealistic the longer you teach, but I hold on to

> what I want to do with them. That's still there intact, if not stronger than ever.

Marie explains that in her DAS classroom problems are solved quite naturally. The students are aware of what is going on, and what their responsibilities are within the structure of the classroom. She ponders her own responsibility and how her own actions can affect the children and herself either positively or negatively. Marie holds to the principle that without any responsibilities then there are no rights. She says:

> People can't just have rights and not the other. It won't work. So it's a perfect balance where there's individual choice, but … the individual choice doesn't outweigh the choice of the group, where there's individual say and opinions, but your opinion doesn't [outweigh] the opinion of the group. And, if the opinion of the group is that we are doing this and we're doing it this way, then you have to compromise … because that's how it works in a big group; you can't have your say all the time … so that's a skill to me, and it's a skill that brings you to responsible citizenship.

Several years after her time at DAS, Marie founded Voice Integrative School (VIS), a privately run, not-for-profit school in Toronto that focuses on global education. The school continues to evolve.

From the phase 2 interview with Lori (2004):

Like Marie, Lori taught at DAS during the early years of her career. Some ten years later, she filled us in on her work after DAS:

> It was a big, big transition to go from an alternative school to the regular stream. It was a huge shock. I mourned DAS for a year … I thought I had made a really huge mistake. I felt

like a fish out of water, but slowly, I've managed to integrate … I feel really fortunate that that was the foundation of my teaching career. I learned a lot of things [at DAS]. I learned a lot about children. I learned a lot about parents … [and] had fabulous colleagues along the way … those kids were my "pre-Kate" children. So before having my own child … I was invested in them emotionally much more than I am with my students now, just by virtue of the fact that I have my own child and all those feelings go for her, rightly so. So when I think back to [DAS kids] … I love them.

I feel very fortunate to have started at DAS and to have met the wonderful, kind, child-centered people that I met, who really loved children and who were completely dedicated to making the lives of children as rich and as safe as they could.

After that first year [after DAS] where I was just so unhappy and thinking, what the heck was I doing … and leaving my baby for the first time, going back to work full-time, and it was not a happy year for me … but I've grown accustomed to it and I like my school.

You know for these kids, they didn't have the language of conflict resolution. They didn't know how to talk beyond blaming. And so, the first, the beginning of the year it's about trying to listen to what people need, being able to say what you actually need from the other person, rather than blaming … and regurgitating all the past, you know conflicts, that they've had in the past. So there's a lot of work to be done.

But I tend to talk to kids about problems that affect all of us, in a whole group forum, and that's always interesting too because … it's nice to have all of these philosophies, but then you have thirty-five personalities who need to be able to sit, fit on a carpet, and be able to listen to one another and not interrupt … and learn how to be respectful to one another and … [with their] varying levels of ability, to speak to each other about their feelings and speak in a respectful way about their perspectives, and that kind of thing. So that's how I handle conflict.

> How I handle conflict in the general school population when I'm out on duty in the halls or in the stairwell is that I'm fairly clear about what I expect, and respect is the big one for me, and being kind to one another, not walking through a doorway and letting the door slam [into] the person … similar to DAS, we don't have a lot of physical problems at our school but, you know, there's exclusion and that kind of thing, that you [have to handle] with children all the time. So I often say, "You can't say you can't play," (Paley, 1993). Even though [this school has] 430 students … it's not okay for you to exclude somebody, but it happens.

Lori tells us that at her new school she felt overwhelmed by things that got in the way when she wanted to follow through with a problem, unlike DAS, where she took for granted that everybody was invested in solving problems. At DAS she could casually and easily ask another adult to cover her class while she worked with kids to resolve an issue. At her new school she came to the following realization:

> Something has to give. I can't leave a class of thirty-five students unattended while I deal with two students who are having a conflict. Where at DAS, I could say to somebody, "Could you cover my class because I need to talk to … to work through this problem with these two kids." When I was having a "girl issue" at the very beginning of the year, there were other players from other classrooms, so I had to go and talk to their teachers about releasing them and how much time they would be willing to allow for that problem to be rehashed and solved because one of the things at DAS was the problem isn't solved until everybody feels that it is. And some people need a lot of time.
>
> What I find with kids [who] come to me is that I really have to spend a good six weeks integrating them into my

> set of expectations, because I want to get down to some fun learning and have some creative interactions with them. But unless they have some ability to manage their own behavior and keep themselves organized, and take responsibility for their own learning and how they interact with other people … that becomes impossible.
>
> So, my indoctrination process is the first six weeks of school. And you know, you have to review … mathematics is a building block, language is a building block. But they come [to] you from all over the place. So, you have kids who are skilled in math, some strands of math and not in others, so it's all over the map. I hope that what I teach and what I believe, and how I feel about children and parents and teachers working together is the right thing, but who knows? I mean, what's to say that a child coming out of my classroom gets a better education than a child coming out of somebody else's classroom? I think that they come out of my classroom thinking a little bit more, questioning a little bit more. Feeling like they have a right to say what they don't like, knowing how to say what they don't like and in a respectful way … feeling like they have power as human beings to make change in the world.

Lori talks about incorporating math and writing with other aspects of learning that she considers important:

> I can give them those skills in conjunction with what I think is a humane education … I bring my own personality to this deal. And I'm strong-minded … I have strong expectations of myself and of the kids … they have to care about other people's feelings. They can't be selfish or self-centered … learning is an exciting adventure. And if you don't … understand something, you have the right to say to your teacher, "I don't understand this and you need to help me."
>
> I like the fact that our kids … you know, sometimes, I'm tired and I want to brush them off, but they don't let me. I think that's good. I think it's important that they make sure that I hear them.

Lori and Marie were key contributors to the DAS peacemaking journey. It is important to pay close attention to their words and to learn how they have gone on to do their innovative work in subsequent years.

9

Tragedies and Question Marks

Tashi knew from an early age that it was okay to grow his thick brown hair down to his waist. He had a difficult time learning to read, but he worked hard and became good at it. He was strong, articulate, and knew how to speak his mind. He took a lot of risks.

My home phone rang extra early on a Monday morning in 2008. It was Ann Lacey with the tragic news. Tashi, one of the first serious DAS peacemakers, was dead. It happened in British Columbia following extensive treatment in a center where he had been invited to stay on to become one of the teachers. An accidental overdose. There would be a notice in the paper and a celebration of his life on Saturday morning. Ann and I agreed to meet just before the service.

In 1988, when he was in 1st grade, Tashi was already a teacher. He taught peacemaking before we teachers really understood that peacemaking was taking hold with our students. One evening at a parent meeting, Tashi stepped forward to explain it, while we adults were still stumbling to find the right words for what we were trying to accomplish with the children. Tashi just took over the meeting. He announced that he had begun to gather groups of kids in the park near his home to help them resolve conflicts. As he fielded parents' questions, we teachers learned details from him about what was changing in our (their) playground at recess.

From discussions with Tashi then and again seven years later, when he was in 8th grade and I interviewed him about his valiant and successful journey with reading, I learned a lot, or at least I thought I did.

For me something had shattered. Tashi was gone and so was a certainty I had been clinging to. This is a larger-than-Tashi story; it's about the vulnerabilities of certain children, maybe all children. Did we DAS adults participate in making this boy too trusting of the world? Did we do that to other children? Did we set kids up to expect safety in the danger zone that is the 21st Century?

At the memorial service, Tashi's grandfather told a story about Tashi as a little boy jumping off the back of the family boat, so certain of his own well-being that he ignored warnings that he might not be able to catch up and climb aboard. "This time," said his grandfather in tears at the church podium, "this time Tashi didn't make it back."

Until that moment I had not fully understood the risks. I still grieve. We must ask the question: can teachers become too optimistic? Is it a betrayal to encourage children to hope too much, trust too easily, be too confident, take the kinds of risks that enable us all to learn and face hard truths?

Children as Peacemakers is on the verge of a "next phase" with a small group of those former DAS children, who are now themselves in their early years of work with young people. Some of them are classroom teachers. This is happening at a time in history when we have no choice but to confront issues of life and death, as we think with children about student-to-student conflicts.

Just this past fall in 2014 (in the week that I write this) a nineteen-year-old high school student in Toronto, described in the media as a "very, very, nice guy" and "a peacemaker" was stabbed to death in the hallway of his high school when he tried to break up a fight among other boys. His name was Hamid. He was not Toronto born, he did not go to DAS; he was in fact a fairly recent immigrant, who witnesses report was trying to do "the right thing."

So we have to pause and think seriously about whether or not peacemaking techniques should still be encouraged in our schools. What are we to do when there is barbarism among our youth? Do we cease teaching negotiation skills and social responsibility because this can embolden children to step into danger? Do we continue to teach peacemaking skills and connect this with instruction in self-defense techniques? Do we instead teach children that it's acceptable to look on and do nothing, and thereby perpetuate the myth that there is such a thing as an innocent bystander? Where do we turn for wisdom in a season when the armies of so many nations are confronting the ultimate threats against international safety and justice? How do we advise our teachers and our students in the face of local and worldwide atrocity?

It is chilling to write this book about child peacemakers as troops from around the world amass to wage war in the cause of peace. How are children to comprehend this deepest of all contradictions? How are they to understand their social responsibilities? What are they to see as their options? Whom are they to trust?

10

Into the Present: On to the Future

I wanted to bring together a group of the early DAS students for a phase 3 of this project, to find out how their childhood experiences are influencing their adult lives. DAS students have dispersed, and the first step was to find contact information and email them. In recent years, I have been in touch with those who participated in conferences we hosted in Toronto. Others have turned up in my classes at York University. Quite a few gave us interviews for the second phase of the project (2003-2007). Occasionally we hear from a former student to ask for a copy of the 2001 documentary or just to say, "Hi." Sometimes there is a double-take followed by a "Hello!" at the public library or on the subway or in the waiting room of the eye doctor. DAS kids and their parents are everywhere, doing important work and wanting to re-connect, celebrate achievements together, and support each other during sad times.

With help from my graduate assistants, I find email addresses. I send messages to a long list of these kids-grown-up inviting them for brunch and conversation on December 7, 2014. All but two or three on my list respond, saying that they want to take part in phase 3 of the project. Some are able to attend the brunch. Others are far away and ask how they might participate from a distance. Many offer photographs, resumes and writing.

We meet at my home on December 7, 2014 and again on March 22, 2015. A small number attend including Alice, Caitlin, Elli, Molly, Nataleah, Savannah, and Sonia. We audiotape the discussion on December 7 at my dining room table. On March 22, 2015 we videotape discussion and interviews. Many send pieces of writing, photographs, and updates on their current lives and work. Here are some examples of their contributions to this collection:

Naomi and Abraham

Naomi lives in Europe; she designs, sews, and works in the clothing industry. She writes:

> What I learned most in the peacemaking project was that other children thought and interpreted things differently from the way I did. To learn at such a young age that the world is seen differently by every person has been a huge part of making me a more caring and understanding adult. At five-years-old you are such a self-centered being. The peacemaking project really helped kids to understand someone else's problems.

> I may not use the formal peacemaking structure that I learned as a kid, but I find the skills are still used now. When I am angry with someone I take time to calm down, then once I'm able to talk reasonably, I discuss with that person how the situation made both of us feel, and how we could better handle this in the future. I remember how rewarding and mature we felt when able to solve problems [with] each other without needing a teacher to help us.

Josh grown up

Naomi's big brother Josh was one of the very first peacemakers. He was the strong-minded kindergarten boy who ran meetings in a tire swing on the DAS playground, the boy who at age seven came to the York University campus in 1991 to speak about peacemaking to teacher candidates. Josh is now an organic farmer in Ontario. He has a child, a little boy. Josh won't be able to attend the gathering, but he wants to know other ways to contribute. Their parents live in Toronto. They give me photographs. We interviewed Naomi and Josh as teenagers in their family kitchen. (see the website *www.childrenaspeacemakers.ca*)

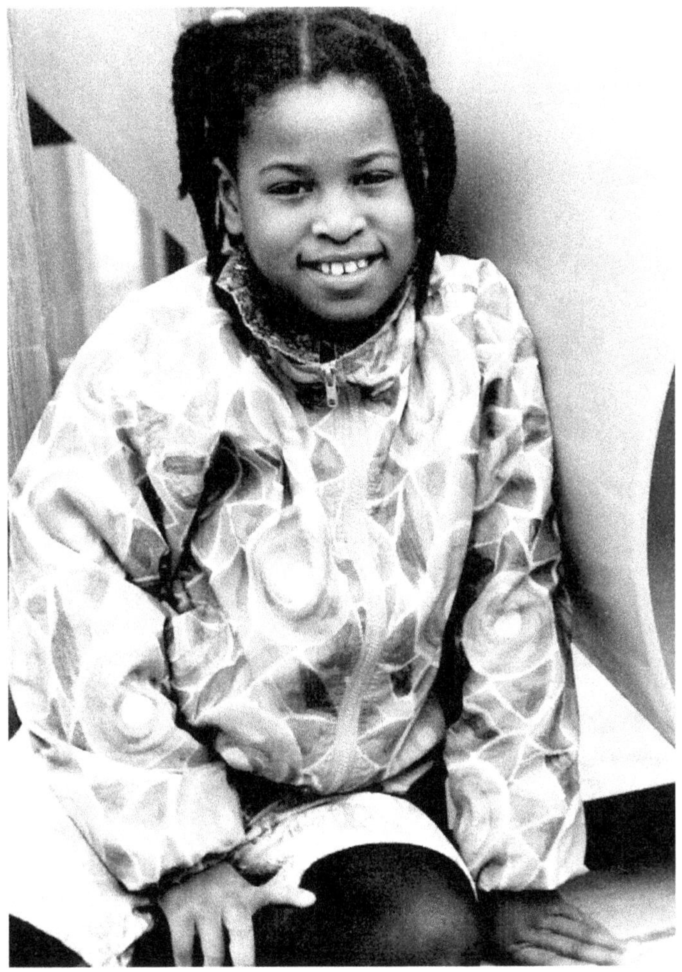

Nataleah

Nataleah is at the table, and as always, expands the discussion with her ideas and her honesty. We have interviewed her more recently than the others. She has contributed a great deal to the writing of this book. Her voice is prominent in Chapter 2.

Corey at DAS and grown up

Corey lives in Montreal. She is an accomplished professional musician. We interviewed her just over ten years ago in 2004, as she was about to leave Toronto to attend McGill University. In that interview (see the website *www.childrenaspeacemakers.ca*), Corey speaks movingly about how DAS was a place for her, and her mother Cathy, and all kinds of families with their own life styles and gender differences, to be open about who they were/are. Corey and Cathy respond enthusiastically to my email. They send me photos.

Sonia

Sonia is also at the table. She was a child participant in the early study (1993-1996). Since university, she has traveled and lived abroad, worked as an artisan, and is now exploring ways to pursue her interests in various graduate programs. More significantly, she tells me she is trying to discover a space, a community, where social justice work is the central focus. In 2015, Sonia reflects on the DAS experience. She writes:

> I am proud to say that I attended DAS for my elementary school years. I remember peacemaking fondly, both as I participated in it and as I witnessed it among peers. It was undoubtedly challenging, however it was just the norm of what we did: address issues and try to work through them to the best of everyone's abilities.
>
> In retrospect (and after having seen footage of some actual peacemaking moments involving myself and my peers), I am extremely impressed with our capacity as young children to implement the tools of peacemaking. These tools of conflict resolution and peer mediation, I believe, had us functioning at high levels of emotional intelligence and maturity. We were practicing being our authentic selves while exercising reason and empathy to mediate through our issues.
>
> As beneficial as DAS and peacemaking was, I also feel it set us up for some difficulties. Mainly: the overall challenge of being in an environment that is so specialized and then going out of that environment and trying to function within new norms. I think this happened in two regards. The first was the experience of leaving the peacemaking environment and entering another occurred throughout our years at DAS. This was simply the fact that we had to leave the classroom at the end of every day as well as over the weekends to go home.
>
> Home was another environment where a complete set of … norms existed, or at least a re-prioritization of them was [our] reality. The second, the experience of leaving the peacemaking environment and entering another, occurred when leaving the school altogether, either due to graduation or changing schools. This had us going into a new school environment that came with a whole new set of norms, which

> were probably not as conducive to the peacemaking process as learned at DAS.
>
> The challenge of adhering to different norms, I believe, was further exacerbated by the fact that we were young. As children we were vulnerable to authority and most likely quite impressionable, in any environment that we occupied. This may have led many of us to diminish and/or not practice what we learned … maybe even to the point of forgetting what we learned.
>
> Without a doubt, life after DAS has had me feeling uncomfortable. DAS taught and nurtured a language and a manner of being that is not commonly known or valued in the larger parts of our society. There have been countless instances in which I felt I was in a world where I could not practice my peacemaking skills. Or maybe I was in such a world, but I missed an opportunity to exercise those skills.
>
> More and more however, I catch myself occupying spaces in which I can apply my skills … no matter the difficulties, that DAS may have set me up for later on in life, I believe that the peacemaking environment has [affected] me positively. No matter how much life I have lived since DAS, I will always have those memories and experiences that are part of my nature. I am forever grateful that my parents elected DAS as my elementary school.

Alice is at the table. She attended DAS as a young child; she graduated from Trent University with an honors BA in Political Studies. Later, Alice sends me a bio. She writes that she has worked in retail and in the field of restorative justice. She explains that some of her work has been with youth and with a YWCA Court Support Program that supports women who find themselves [caught] in the justice system. In 2015 Alice reflects:

> Since phase 2 of the DAS Project my life has changed pretty

> drastically. In 2004 when we filmed the 10-years-later … I was living in a group home and struggling with some anxiety issues. Shortly after the second filming I joined a group called Leave Out Violence (LOVE), a youth violence prevention and intervention program that uses restorative justice, alternative conflict resolution, empowerment and creativity to help youth who have been affected by violence in some way to embrace their stories and help to change their communities.
>
> I volunteered for LOVE from 2004 to 2011 and have recently joined their alumni project mentorship and advocacy project. In 2008 I graduated from the Student Secondary Alternative School. I also sat on the steering Hub for the Trent Queer Collective.

Savannah wrote to me in 2012 while she was studying to become a teacher. She wanted to talk. We met for coffee. Since that year Savannah has been working as a substitute teacher on long-term assignments. She attends our first phase 3 gatherings and brings her insights and deep questions to my dining room table.

Savannah attended DAS as a student from 1st – 6th grade. She says that to her it was just a "normal school," where she solved conflicts peacefully with her friends, and didn't get made fun of for wearing "extensive amounts of orthodontic gear." It wasn't until after DAS that she realized how incredibly lucky she was to have been there. Currently an arts [dance] educator and elementary school teacher, Savannah weaves much of her learning from DAS into her professional life. She strives to create a community within her classroom, where every student feels valued and has a voice. She envisions a future school system where a school like DAS is the standard, not the exception, where this type of education is accessible to all children and not only to "lucky kids" like her. (Interviews with Savannah and her lifelong friend Christine are on the *www.*

childrenaspeacemakers.ca website.)

Christine writes back to me. Her emails say that she wants to participate in the phase 3 project from her home in Newfoundland and will be in touch soon.

Hanna lives in Montreal. On the day of our gathering she will be singing with her choir and her father Rick will be there with her. They would like to join us on Skype, which didn't work out for the first gathering, but might at a later time. Hanna and her father are both in the documentary in a playground peacemaking with Molly and others (described in chapter 6). Hanna is also in the kindergarten building day scene in 1995 where the Bank of Montreal becomes a point of dispute with Maya. Hanna's mother gives me photographs.

Hanna and her family

Hanna was born and raised in Toronto. She attended DAS from pre-K – 3rd grade, before transferring to a gifted program to complete elementary school. She attended Ursula Franklin Academy for high school, a small public school of high academic ranking with a social justice and community engagement focus. During the time from DAS until the end of high school, Hanna also attended classes at and later joined the company of Canadian Children's Dance Theatre (now Canadian Contemporary Dance Theatre). Interested in science, Hanna went on to complete a B.Sc. in biology with a neuroscience minor from the University of Guelph. This April she will be completing her master's degree in neuroscience at McGill University. Her research focuses on understanding the developmental origins of schizophrenia using a postnatal lesion model in rats, particularly looking into parvalbumin neurons in the prefrontal cortex and thalamus. Hanna writes:

> My fondest memories of DAS are the people: the teachers who really cared and invested in the students, and my peers, some of whom remain my best friends today. Of course, peacemaking ties into everyday peacemaking … I do remember a "scandal" when I was in grade 3 that required the entire class to cooperate in the peacemaking circle. The scandal involved gossip that had been going around about two students. Having a space where the students could share their feelings under the supervision of a neutral moderator was very valuable.
>
> I feel as though peacemaking made me more empathetic to the people around me, fostered a desire and ability to talk through problems reasonably, and most of all taught me to listen to and respect people's feelings.

Molly and her mom Anna both respond to my emails. Molly plans to attend the gathering, but at the last minute has to cancel. She plans to come to the next one. Anna sends photos. In their phase 2 interview, Molly and Anna talked about the value of having been part of a community at DAS where they could be themselves, talk openly and comfortably about their multiple mom family, and

Molly and her mother Anna

know they were as supported as all other families at DAS. Here is a small excerpt from that interview we did with them in their own backyard in 2004:

> **Question:** When you think about DAS—when you think yourself back to grade 6, but even earlier if you can—when you were talking about your family or bringing things in from home, did you feel comfortable about bringing up issues or describing your family or sharing, do you think you felt as comfortable as you were entitled to feel, or were there other things you wish had been a little bit different?
>
> **Molly:** I was completely comfortable with talking about my family. I never met any issues with that actually. People thought it was really cool that I had four moms. They were like oh wow, you are the luckiest person in the world and Fathers' Day comes around I'm like ah I get to take a break. So then mom's day comes and I'm like ah I have to get four cards done, and it wasn't anything. It wasn't any big deal, nobody really minded. Nobody thought about it as anything but normal.
>
> **Question:** So you didn't have to explain yourself, you felt people understood?
>
> **Molly:** Yeah, pretty much. The interesting thing was there

> were adults that didn't seem to get it and then as you get older a lot of older kids who didn't seem to get it, but it was never the kids that really seemed to care ... it was wow that's so different! It was just adults mostly.

Now in 2015, Molly's mom Anna writes that she has been questioning authority and confronting the abuse of power since she was teenager in Milton, Ontario. She has a long history in the women's anti-violence community in Toronto and is the proud lesbian mom of two wonderful young adults and a grandmother of one. She has been teaching in the Assaulted Women's and Children's Counselor/Advocate program at George Brown College since 2000, and manages a program at the college called Women Transitioning to Trades and Employment. Anna also facilitates workshops and courses in community settings with adult learners. She is a long time member of the Toronto Police Accountability Coalition [*http://www.tpac.ca*] and the Groundswell Community Justice Trust Fund [*http://groundswellfund.ca*], and she publishes the

Molly

weekly email newsletter, *Rise Up! News and Events.* Anna writes:

> I don't have a lot of specific memories to share, only because I have a terrible memory.
>
> I'm not sure if Molly will have a chance to write, as she is very busy with her master's studies these days. The experience at DAS was a wonderful one for her, and she made friends there that she continues to have strong relationships with 20 years later. I believe the peacemaking program is largely responsible for this—the kids in her group learned to communicate and grow with each other through situations that could have resulted in lasting hurt and separation.
>
> She learned skills in her early years that she has honed over the years, and she's developed into a thoughtful and well-spoken adult who has excellent analytic skills. And her classmates are the same. Our son had a different experience, as he came to DAS in grade 2 or 3, and didn't get the same kind of early learning of the peacemaking skills. I wish we had heard about the school earlier!

Pandora lives in London, England. She has two children and is working to complete her doctorate in art history. As a 2nd grader, she drew the picture of a creature who came to be called The Peaceosaurus. Her drawing remains the DAS logo and is immortalized on the cover of the book (by the same name) written by the first four peacemakers (1988). She and I had lunch together at the British Library in December 2013. She remembers the picture but doesn't remember drawing it the first time.

Pandora writes that she was born and raised in Toronto, and is now based in London UK where she is completing a PhD in the History of Art at University College London (UCL). She teaches modern and contemporary art and display practices at UCL, and in museums and galleries throughout London. She has exhibited as an artist and curator across Canada and has presented her research internationally.

Her recent publications include chapters in *Framing the Ocean, 1700 to Present: The Sea as Social Space in Western Art* (Ashgate, 2014), *Ben Judd: Communion* (Black Dog, 2014), *Coral: Something Rich and Strange* (Liverpool University Press, 2013), and *Contesting Bodies and Nation in Canadian History* (University of Toronto Press, 2013). She has written for periodicals including *C Magazine, Canadian Art* and *MAP*. In 2010 she received the Canadian Art Foundation Writing Prize. Previously she worked as part of the curatorial team at the Walter Phillips Gallery, the Banff Centre, where she co-curated an exhibition on sound and ecology in radio art. She holds an MA in Art History and Curatorial Studies from York University, Toronto, and a BFA from Concordia University, Montreal. Pandora says she applies her alternative education and peacemaking ethos to her teaching and to raising her two young sons, "for better or for worse."

Maya has been hard to track down. Finally she has seen and responded to an email from me. She says she is very interested in participating in the phase 3 project. She has just returned from travel, and she will be in touch soon. She is searching for photographs to send me. I hope that an interview with her and some written thoughts will follow. If this works out, her interview will appear on the website.

Zak wrote to me a while ago. He was running a peacemaking program at a large downtown elementary school in Toronto. He wanted to talk about this with me. We have corresponded, but have not yet found a time to meet; I'm confident that eventually we will.

Nathalie was one of the first four peacemakers, at eight years

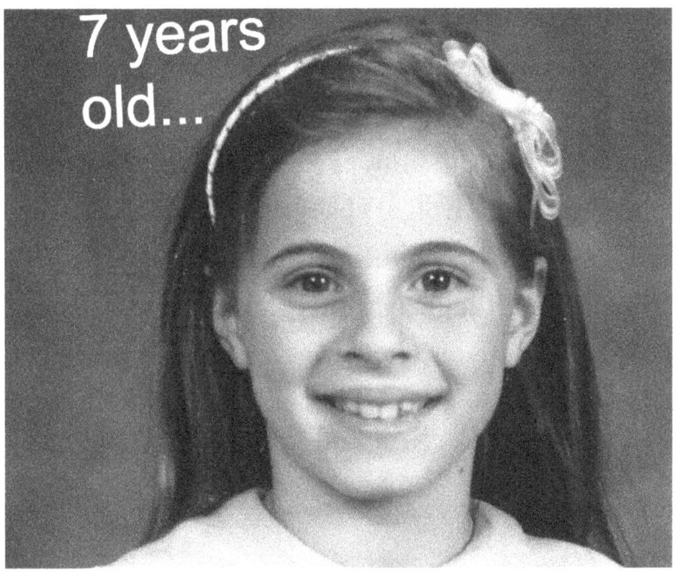

Nathalie

old one of the four co-authors of *The Peaceosaurus* book. She is an elementary teacher. She has taught in Portugal and now in Thailand. She sends me a link to her PowerPoint, where she explains and showcases her peacemaking work with children in her own classroom. She writes to me (with permission to quote from her email):

> My father always told me the Peaceosaurus would stay with me my whole life … I never really believed him … now as a teacher working abroad … I am amazed at how often I reference this book … how often I use the skills I learned as a young child at DAS and put it into my practice in the classroom. We have the Peaceosaurus on our bookshelf … we have watched the film … my children are peacemakers :).

Caitlin, Tallulah, Ilyssa, Alyssa, and Jessica have been in my classes at York University and have helped me explain peacemaking to teacher candidates.

Caitlin became a high school teacher. As one of the first DAS peacemakers, Caitlin co-authored *The Peaceosaurus* (1988). She and her sister Lesley came to DAS before we began the video research. Caitlin is a couple of years older than others at the gathering and is meeting most of them for the first time. Nonetheless, conversation flows easily, unstoppably, seamlessly, as if these young people had been in each other's lives everyday all along. They speak the same language. They remember teachers together. They open up with each other. They laugh. They shed some tears. They ponder issues. We tape. They don't hold back, and thus in many moments, I hear the words, "This is off the record." They astonish me with the level of trust that they reach (or re-capture) so quickly.

Jessica and her grandfather

Jessica grown up

Jessica has returned from England after her first year of teaching. She writes:

> I never planned on being a teacher. I was going to be a Linguist, but then I became involved in a Socio-Linguistic study on the effects of cultural myths on the development of social reasoning in young children, and I ended up working with these amazing kindergarten children and seeing what incredible things they were capable of with just a little help, and I fell in love with helping them.
>
> For most of my life, I didn't realize the impact that the Peacemakers Project had had on me, but once I became a teacher, I realized how it had shaped my understanding of young

> children and their capacity for reason and problem solving skills. As adults, especially as teachers and parents, we can fall into the trap of trying to "fix" everything for our little darlings. Obviously, we know best, we have years of experience and knowledge, and they are just children.
>
> Peacemakers allowed me to learn, as a child, and remember, as an adult, that often children are much better suited to understanding and solving their own problems, and that sometimes we need to step back and let a peer, who understands the underlying issues and feelings that only a five, or six, or ten-year-old can have, unsnarl this knot that seems so straightforward to us and yet we can't seem to find the ends.
>
> Today I work with autistic and other challenged children doing intensive sensory-cognitive language remediation, and every day I must tell myself not to underestimate them, to acknowledge their expertise in a subject [where] I'm an outsider … in being a kid.

Elli brings her energy and experiences to my table. Two videotaped interviews with Elli and her mother Sharon (one in 1994 when Elli was in 1st grade, and the other in 2005 when she was just about to graduate from high school) are discussed in chapter 7 of this book, and can be seen on the *www.childrenaspeacemakers.ca* website. Now, Elli shares current information about herself. She writes that she is a local mindfulness practitioner and teacher. She has recently spent a year as the International Program Coordinator for Wake Up Schools, a global initiative to cultivate mindfulness in education, initiated by Nobel Peace Prize nominee, renowned Zen Master, scholar and peace activist Thich Nhat Hanh.

Elli's ongoing work with Plum Village focuses on a holistic approach to education, working simultaneously with teachers, students, parents and administrators to build sustainable inclusive communities. She has organized retreats and facilitated workshops in Bhutan, India, Germany, Canada, UK and USA. In 2013 she was part of Thich Nhat Hanh's North American teaching tour, offering retreats and workshops at centers across Canada and the United States, including workshops at The World Bank and Google headquarters. She has recently worked in Toronto, Canada with the organization *Me to We*, implemented a school-wide mindfulness program for a downtown elementary school, and has given guest lectures for teacher candidates at University of Toronto/OISE and York University's Regent Park Site.

Elli holds a master's degree from York University's Environmental Studies program, focused on the practical use and implementation of mindfulness in Western education. She has also worked as a producer in the film industry, and she has used this experience to create several short documentary films exploring mindfulness as a secular tool to combat issues of workplace burnout and stress. She is honored to be a grant-making advisor for the Pollination Project, a foundation that gives seed grants to individual change makers all over the world. Elli grew up in the world of education and mindfulness, attending her first retreat at the age of ten. She is dedicated to the cultivation of a compassionate and healthy society, and through her work she hopes to continue walking a path that leads there.

In 2014 Elli and Sharon and I are invited to give a presentation together in the teacher education program at the University of Toronto/OISE. Soon after I invite Elli and Sharon to give a presentation in my York University classes.

Many educators want a "formula," a prescription, a set curriculum for peacemaking. It doesn't work that way. DAS kids I interviewed tended to make fun of or criticize the peacemaking or conflict resolution programs in schools they attended after DAS. They know that it is more effective, more life changing, when it is "organic," "authentic," "real," though these words are all inadequate to describe the development of social skills, empathy, and ethical sense among people who truly want to resolve (or preserve with respect) their differences. Former DAS students understand. I believe that the peacemaking legacy is secure in their capable hands.

Emily's drawing of peacemakers

Epilogue: An Orderly Seder

With so many strands of experience braided together in this book, I look back across the banquet that has been my forty-year teaching life. I breathe in the amiable scents of my sunny ground floor apartment and exhale on the count of eight in a meditation exercise that is supposed to help a person relax. I write on my Mac Air at three in the morning at my mother's dark cherry wood dining table. The table matches my newish floor and offers a fresh sense of compatibility with my parents, who are gone. After many years of busy family life, I am a widow, living alone, contemplating retirement.

I plan a Passover Seder. I assemble friends and family, and I try to figure out some new ways to celebrate. My daughter Keira, now an adult, helps me prepare. Family drive here from Michigan, Leslie cooks the lamb chops. She and my brother Joe buy schnapps at the duty free at the Detroit Windsor border. The brand they choose bears our family name. I make a huge pot of chicken soup using the recipe from our cousin's cookbook (Sokolov, 1989).

Matzah balls light as air are my specialty. I always make too many. Gefilte fish from the market will do; I never learned how to do that part, and I don't want to start now. Matzah, horseradish, and shaved cinnamon apples with sweet wine and walnuts are Keira's specialty. Her haroset, constructed into little brick and mortar sandwiches, are a key part of the ritual that reminds us of who we are still trying to be, even though so many of our relatives are departed, dispersed, detached, and different from one another.

My husband Adrian has died, leaving the head of the table to my discretion. We make the Seder collaborative; it doesn't require a leader. A facilitator and a full table is all we need. We read from a reform Haggadah and skip the parts that make us uncomfortable; the text has grown more woman friendly with language less gendered, the anti-Egyptian passages still make us squirm, but they are mainly true, our ancestors *were* slaves many thousands of years ago in Egypt. We will giggle as we suck the wine from our fingers during the part about the plagues—the frogs, the locusts. We like to savor our traditions and remember what it meant to be treasured children squeezed between relatives at a noisy Seder table, Grandfather (a Zaida) at the head with a special wine glass waiting for the Prophet Elijah to steal a sip and stagger away to the next house unseen. At the ancient table recreated in 21st Century style are disparate forces that conspire with tradition out of commitment, respect, habit, and the human need for community, to combine old and new flavors, bring them to life, and bind us together.

I will open two kinds of wine, the sweet Manishewitz, which carries some of our deepest of memories, and some dry Israeli wines to please our modern taste buds. We will bring relevant questions and harmony to our Seder table, while all over the world troubled people of so many religions and skin colors and philosophical beliefs and political perspectives suffer and struggle, some trying to negotiate peace as others load their rifles. I hold to a belief that *Raising Peacemakers* offers legitimate hope. I summon the small voices of the reflective young people who asked those serious questions in Chapter 1 of this book:

Do you want to solve the problem?

Do you want to solve it with us or the teachers?

Do you agree to listen?

No plugging your ears?

No interrupting?

No arguing back and forth?

No stepping on toes?

No denying?

There are still so many roads, borders, and barriers to cross. Let us double-cross our arms, clasp fingers in a group handshake with the next generation, and keep trying to Peacemake.

References

Burrell, C., Nyman, D., Filmus, D., Herve-Azevedo, N. (1988). *The Peaceosaurus*. D.A.S.osaurus Press, Toronto.

Fine, E., Lacey, A., Baer J. (1995). *Children as Peacemakers*. Portsmouth, NH: Heinemann.

Fine, E. (1997). *Learning the Language of Peacemaking: Researching the Early Moments*, Canadian Children: Journal of the Canadian Association for Young Children, Fall, Vol. 22/2 pages 18-22.

Fine, E. (2003) *Storytime*, Talking Points, Whole Language Umbrella, National Council of Teachers of English, 15 (1): 25-26

Paley, V. G. (1993). *You Can't Say You Can't Play*. Cambridge, MA: Harvard University Press.

Sadalla, G. Halligan, J., & Holmberg, M. (1990). Conflict Resolution: An elementary school curriculum. San Francisco, CA: Community Board Program.

Sokolov, R., (1989). *The Jewish-American Kitchen*, Stewart, Tabori, & Chang, New York.

WEB LINKS:

Esther Fine Peacemaking Research Website: *http://www.childrenaspeacemakers.ca*

Groundswell Community Justice Trust Fund: *http://www.groundswellfund.ca*

Marie Lardino: *http://www.voiceintegrativeschool.com/*

Roberta King (King Squires Films Ltd.) *http://www.kingsquirefilms.com/*

Rise Up! News and Events. Anna Willats—weekly email newsletter. *http://weareontario.ca/index.php/rise-up-toronto-news-events-feb17-2013/*

Toronto Police Accountability Coalition: *http://www.tpac.ca*

FILMS:

Documentary: *Life at School: The DAS Tapes.* (2001). King Squire Films Ltd., Toronto, Canada

Film for children: *The Peaceosaurus.* (2011). Barb Taylor, Coyle Productions. Toronto, Canada (based on the book with the same title, The Peaceosaurus, by DAS 3rd graders Caitlin Burrell, Diego Filmus, Daniel Nyman, and Nathalie Herve-Azevedo, 1988). Can be seen on the website *www.childrenaspeacemakers.ca*

About the Author: Esther Sokolov Fine

Esther Sokolov Fine is an Associate Professor in the Faculty of Education at York University, in Toronto, Canada, where she has taught since 1991. Before coming to York, she was an elementary teacher with the Toronto Board of Education. There, she taught in downtown public housing communities and alternative programs, including four years at the Downtown Alternative School (DAS). The book *Children as Peacemakers* (1995), which she co-authored with teachers Ann Lacey and Joan Baer, presents a history of the Downtown Alternative School and tells about the early years of peacemaking. Reflecting on her own early life, Esther writes:

> When I was a child I did not picture myself as a teacher. I did imagine growing up and having more freedom and a voice with which to spark changes. I was forever

looking for somewhere else to be as I rode my rusty blue tricycle around and around the block hoping to get lost. In my starchy blue dress (mid-city Detroit—Fitzgerald School—1940s), I poked under the ink well, caused a nasty spill, and was moved to a special chair next to the teacher's desk.

I didn't know how to play on a playground, so mostly I wandered around waiting for recess to be over. Occasionally I ventured partway up the jungle gym, but mostly I studied the people and the action. I had friends, but we tended to walk and chat rather than run and jump. I couldn't hit a softball. Kickball was not much better. Teachers were strict but friendly, demanding yet compassionate, and for their time, they were probably well informed, progressive, and reasonable. The best part of school was when librarian Mrs. Barnes and some of our homeroom teachers read aloud from wonderful books. The worst part was the long walk home from school, crossing the vacant lot by myself on a narrow path that led to Lilac Street. Bullies lurked there, and sometimes stray dogs. I remember my fear. I remember a snaggle-toothed boy named Roland in a black leather jacket with crisscross zippers. He had wild eyes, a cackle-laugh, and a knife. I remember treading cautiously and quietly with my eyes on the ground, hoping he wouldn't notice me. Sometimes he did. The schoolyard felt safer.

> Many years later, as an elementary schoolteacher, surrounded by playground activity, I was sensitive to kids who seemed uneasy. I was searching for and writing about alternative ways of "doing school." With twelve years of teaching under my belt, much of it in public housing communities, I was invited (by teachers and parents) to join the staff of the Downtown Alternative School. As fairly mild everyday conflicts became a center of attention there, I found myself increasingly able to focus my eyes and ears on people, action, and negotiations. What a journey this has been for me and for those of us who shared in the wonderfully collaborative years of teaching and research that began at that school.

Since 1993 Esther has been engaged in video research with the same group of students, teachers and parents. In this research (largely funded by the Social Sciences and Humanities Research Council of Canada—SSHRC) she and filmmaker Roberta King have watched these children grow up and filmed and interviewed many of them, their families, and their teachers across this 20+ year period. Details and edited film from this work can be seen at *www.childrenaspeacemakers.ca*. A feature documentary, *Life at School: the DAS Tapes*, was launched in 2001.

Esther teaches pre-service and graduate courses in creative writing, literacy, adolescent and children's literature, critical pedagogy, and models (alternative models) of education. She was born in Detroit and attended the University of Michigan where, in 1968, she won a Hopwood Award for fiction. Esther completed her doctoral studies in 1990 at the University of Toronto (Ontario Institute for

Studies in Education) and her MFA in creative writing in 2003 at Vermont College of Fine Arts. Esther has lived in Toronto since the 1960s. She has an adult daughter, Keira, who possesses outstanding social skills and makes her mother proud and grateful every day.

Other Books by Esther Sokolov Fine

Fine, E., Lacey, A., & Baer, J. (1995). *Children as Peacemakers.* Portsmouth, NH: Heinemann

Children's Books:

Fine, E. (1974). *The mushrooming house.* Kids Can Press, Toronto

Fine, E. (1973) *I'm a child of the city.* Kids Can Press, Toronto

Fine, E. (1973). *The double double mirror.* Kids Can Press, Toronto

Children's Books (Supervisory Editor):

Paxton-Beesley, R. (1991). *The food fight*, ta daa. Toronto: Downtown Alternative School

Burrell, C., Herve-Azevedo, N., Nyman, D., & Filmus, D. (1988). *The Peaceosaurus.* Toronto: Downtown Alternative School

www.ingramcontent.com/pod-product-compliance
Ingram Content Group UK Ltd.
Pitfield, Milton Keynes, MK11 3LW, UK
UKHW022002270726
14060UKWH00007B/739/J

9 781942 146193